Cambridge Topics in Geography : seco

Editors Alan R. H. Baker, Emmanuel College, C
Colin Evans, King's College School, Wimbledon

The ecology of agricultural systems

T. P. Bayliss-Smith
Department of Geography, University of Cambridge

Cambridge University Press
Cambridge
New York   Port Chester
Melbourne   Sydney

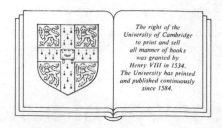

Published by the Press Syndicate of the University of Cambridge
The Pitt Building, Trumpington Street, Cambridge CB2 1RP
40 West 20th Street, New York, NY 10011, USA
10 Stamford Road, Oakleigh, Melbourne 3166, Australia

© Cambridge University Press 1982

First published 1982
Fourth printing 1990

Printed in Great Britain at the University Press, Cambridge

British Library Cataloguing in Publication Data

Bayliss-Smith, T. P.
The ecology of agricultural systems.–(Cambridge topics
in geography series)
1. Agricultural geography
I. Title.
639′.9   S439

ISBN 0 521 23125 6 hard covers
ISBN 0 521 29829 6 paperback

Library of Congress catalogue card number: 82–1132

To David Dykes and Lance Barber, my first teachers

Acknowledgements

Certain chapters in this book were much improved by the helpful suggestions of
B. H. Farmer, John Kingsbury, Betty Meehan, Barbara Neville, Elena Shevchenko,
Graham Smith, and Professor V. Zvorykin. I also thank Michael Young, R. Coe and
D. Markovic who helped with the preparation of maps, diagrams and photographs. The
book was started and finished at St John's College, Cambridge, but the middle portion was
completed while I was a Visiting Fellow in the Research School of Pacific Studies, Australian
National University. I am grateful to both institutions for their support. The photographs in
this book were all taken by the author except Figs. 6.1 and 6.3, which were taken by
B. H. Farmer.

Contents

1 Ecological constraints on agricultural systems

Introduction

My subject in this book is the ecology of agricultural systems, or in other words the relationship between farming practices and the environment that sustains them. My approach to agriculture is different from the usual discussion of climate, soils and crops, but I hope nevertheless to explain some of the processes that underlie its geographical variation. In one short book I cannot possibly cover all aspects of the ecology of agriculture, so instead I focus on the *energy flows* that link the farmer with his crops and animals, so as to discover how the character and magnitude of these flows varies in different cultures.

It was in the 1950s that ecologists first began to analyse the flow of energy in ecosystems, which they defined as environmental units containing plants and animals, integrated by means of interdependent relationships to produce the so-called balance of nature. In the 1960s researchers began to realise that agricultural systems could be analysed also in terms of energy flow, and this work received a boost in the early 1970s when sudden increases in oil prices highlighted the dependence of our 'advanced' methods of farming upon energy from fossil fuels. It became clear that a knowledge of the extent of these supplementary sources of energy might be vitally important in planning for any future energy crisis.

At the same time, work by geographers and anthropologists in less developed parts of the world was beginning to provide detailed information about energy flows in more 'primitive' systems of food production. It is relevant to compare this pre-industrial technology with the very different methods that farmers have adopted in developed countries; there are striking contrasts in efficiency, productivity and ecological stability. In this book I discuss some of this research, in the form of seven different case studies. Each study represents a different strategy for producing food, in response to a different set of ecological and social pressures. The nature of these pressures is discussed in this chapter and in Chapter 2, and the case studies are described in Chapters 3–8.

Some definitions

Every subject generates its own jargon, and the ecology of agriculture is no exception. I shall avoid where possible terms that may be unfamiliar to a geographer, but we must begin by considering the meaning of some words and phrases that will appear repeatedly in these pages.

The first is the term *agricultural system*. A system can be defined at any scale, but I shall be considering systems of food production that exist at rather small scales, those of the village, farm or even individual field. 'Agriculture' will be taken to include the production of food from animals as well as from crops, so that our systems will encompass all of the interactions between man and his food-producing resources, but within small-scale geographical units.

A study of the 'ecology' of such resources implies that the environmental relationships of agriculture (rather than political, social, etc.) will receive most emphasis. However, the focus in this book on energy flows within the agricultural system provides us with an excellent way in which we can view the system in its totality. *Energy* is defined as the capacity to do work, and as such is a highly abstract concept applicable to all sorts of phenomena. Various forms of energy are recognised, including mechanical, chemical, radiant, electrical and nuclear energy. Energy can be transformed from one of its various forms into another, but it can neither be created nor destroyed. But in any transformation there is always a degradation of energy from an organised to a random form, the latter usually being termed *heat energy*. (These last two sentences constitute for the physicist the first two Laws of Thermodynamics.) For example, when petrol is burnt in an engine, or when food is burnt up by respiratory processes in the body, then *chemical energy* is being transformed. In both cases the energy released in the transformation is being used to accomplish work (i.e. the transformation generates *mechanical energy*), with random heat as a by-product.

The various *inputs* into an agricultural system—solar radiation, human labour, the work of machines, applications of fertiliser and herbicide—can all be converted into energy values. Similarly, the *outputs* of the system, the various vegetable and animal products, can also be expressed in energy terms, although the procedure may not be very revealing in cases where the perceived value to man of a product greatly exceeds its actual energy value (compare, for example, strawberries with potatoes). If the inputs and outputs can be quantified in this way then we have a means whereby different kinds of agriculture can be directly compared, at least as regards their intensity, yields, labour productivity, and the levels of welfare that they provide.

'Welfare' is, however, much more than simply a matter of an adequate income, a full stomach, or a satisfactory amount of leisure. Many of the 'outputs' from an agricultural way of life are not easily measurable in scientific terms. Many aspects of agricultural expertise and decision-making are equally intangible, so that it would be unrealistic to expect that because one has analysed the workings of an agricultural system in terms of energy flows one has necessarily explained the reasons for its emergence and persistence as a system of food production. A complete explanation requires much more than a knowledge of how the system functions—although that knowledge is clearly of central relevance to such an explanation.

Solar energy

The light received by the earth from the sun is the ultimate source of all life on our planet. Animals unable to regulate their body temperature, for example invertebrates, fish and reptiles, exploit this solar radiation in a very direct way, since the warmth of their bodies depends upon the warmth of their environment. Unlike reptiles, however, man does not bask in the sunshine primarily in order to absorb heat. In a hot climate

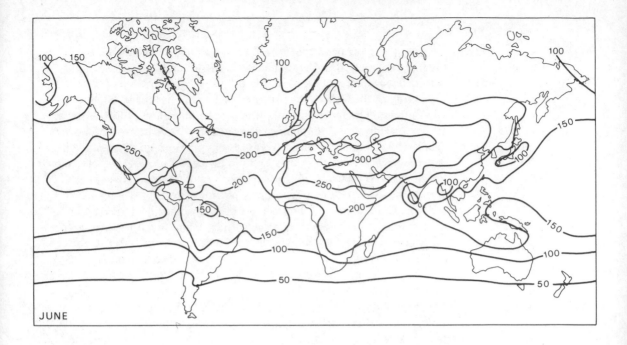

JUNE

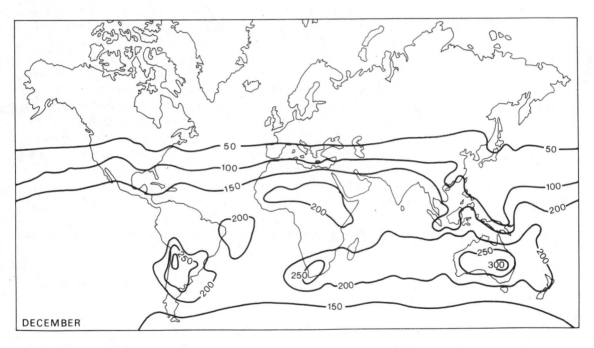

DECEMBER

Fig. 1.1 Geographical variations in the amount of solar radiation received at the earth's surface, June and December. Isopleths show energy in MJ per m^2 per day.

man's dietary energy requirements are in fact not much less than in a cold climate.

The fundamental source of energy for man, as for all animals especially the warm-blooded ones, is the chemical energy from his food. And the ultimate source of this food is plant matter, produced by organisms varying in size from microscopic algae to giant forest trees. This primary production occurs since plants have the capacity to 'fix' solar radiation into chemical matter in the process known as *photosynthesis*. By eating plants, or by eating animals that themselves eat plants, man has therefore always been an indirect exploiter of solar energy.

There are, of course, substantial geographical variations in the amount of solar radiation that is received in different regions (Fig. 1.1). Three factors are important: the altitude of the sun above the horizon, a function of latitude and time of year; day-length, which in high latitudes in particular varies greatly between winter and summer; and cloudiness, which like the sun's altitude determines the proportion of the sun's rays which never reach the earth's surface because they are intercepted within the atmosphere. On a completely clear day about 75% of the radiation reaching the outside of the atmosphere penetrates to the surface, but on an overcast day the proportion falls to about 25%.

This incoming solar radiation is energy in the form of electro-magnetic waves, varying in length and frequency. By international agreement the unit now used to measure all forms of energy is the *joule* (J). The joule is a very small quantity. Expressed in relation to the more familiar energy unit still often used by nutritionists, the calorie, one joule equals 0.239 calories. In this book we shall generally be using the megajoule (MJ) and the gigajoule (GJ):

$$1 \text{ MJ} = 10^6 \text{ J} = 239 \text{ kilocalories}$$
$$1 \text{ GJ} = 10^9 \text{ J} = 239,000 \text{ kilocalories}$$

About 10.5 MJ (2,500 kilocalories) are needed each day by the average man in his diet, in order to maintain the metabolism and tissue replacement of his body.

Examples of the average amount of total radiation received in different parts of the world are shown in Table 1.1. The total amount received per cm^2 per year varies between 0.35 MJ in cloudy cool temperate climates (e.g. Aberystwyth in Wales) to nearly 0.70 MJ in subtropical regions which have a marked summer dry season (e.g. Algeria). In equatorial regions the total solar radiation is usually rather less than in the subtropics, because of the larger amount of cloud often present in the sky. This can be particularly marked in mountainous areas, unless they are in rain shadow. In Ecuador, for example, which is right on the

Table 1.1 Annual and seasonal energy inputs of total solar radiation.

Location	Latitude	Annual input (MJ/cm^2/year)	Seasonal variation Lowest month	Highest month (J/cm^2/day)
Temperate				
Aberystwyth, UK	52°N.	0.35	210	1,880
Tokyo, Japan	36°N.	0.42	630	1,510
Madison, Wisconsin, USA	43°N.	0.50	540	2,220
Subtropical				
Brisbane, Australia	28°S.	0.57	1,150	2,480
Davis, California, USA	39°N.	0.67	750	2,720
Algiers, Algeria	37°N.	0.69	880	2,800
Tropical				
Puyo, Ecuador	1°S.	0.40	1,020	1,240
Manila, Philippines	15°N.	0.54	1,130	1,920
Townsville, Australia	19°S.	0.63	1,580	2,570
Singapore	1°S.	0.65	1,670	2,010

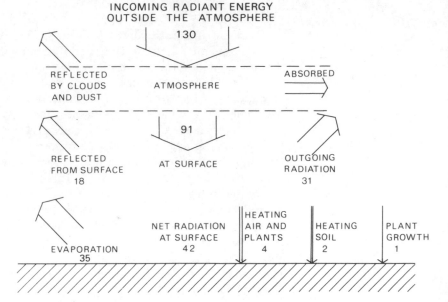

Fig. 1.2 Fate of incoming radiation at the earth's surface, showing quantities typical of a clear sunny day and moist soils (in joules per cm^2 per hour).

equator, the town of Puyo at an altitude of 950 m recorded only 0.40 MJ per cm^2 per year of total radiation, which is little more than that received in Britain.

The data in Table 1.1 also show the large seasonal variation that exists, especially in subtropical and temperate latitudes. At Singapore (1° N) there is only a small difference in cloudiness between different months, and almost no difference in day-lengths. As a result, the average amount of solar radiation received per day is quite similar throughout the year. The difference between maximum and minimum widens when we move into subtropical latitudes, especially when the dry season corresponds with the longer days of summer. At such times rates of solar radiation input are about three times the winter level. In temperate areas, however, they are up to nine times greater: the short days and lack of sunshine in temperate winters mean that even in greenhouses crops such as tomatoes can only be grown with the help of expensive, artificial sunlight.

Interception of solar radiation by vegetation

The amount of solar radiation received at a site is the most fundamental of the various factors which constrain the amount of photosynthetic activity by plants. On the other hand, it is also the factor which the farmer can do least about (unless he sells his farm and moves to a sunnier climate). However, he can do something to ensure that the maximum possible amount of the solar radiation will be intercepted by his crops, and thus will be available for conversion into plant material.

To understand the importance of this factor we must consider what happens to the solar radiation which reaches the earth's surface (Fig. 1.2). Even on a sunny day only about one-third of the incoming solar radiation penetrates the atmosphere, is not reflected or re-radiated back into space, and so is available to carry out various kinds of 'work' at the ground surface. In Fig. 1.2 this category of *net radiation* amounts to 91 joules per cm^2 per hour, and most of it is transformed into latent heat through the evaporation of water (36 J/cm^2/hour). Some is used to warm up the lowest layers of the atmosphere, vegetation and the soil surface (6

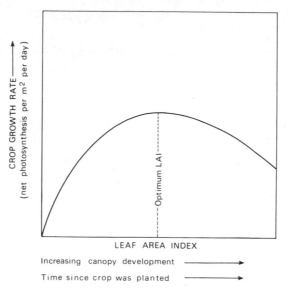

Fig. 1.3 Effect of leaf area index upon the growth rate of a typical agricultural crop.

J/cm²/hour). Only a little (1 J/cm²/hour) is converted into chemical energy as a result of the photosynthetic activity of plants.

Photosynthesis is thus inherently inefficient in its use of solar radiation, converting in our example only about 0.8% of incoming energy at the surface into plant matter. But its efficiency is even lower if the surface is not completely covered with vegetation. The farmer should aim to grow his crop in such a way that the arrangement of its foliage will be optimal for productivity. The amount of foliage is often measured through the *leaf area index*, which simply gives the total leaf area (in cm²) per unit of soil surface (also in cm²). Experiments with many crops have shown that until the plants have grown sufficiently to completely cover the ground surface, much solar radiation will be wasted, falling in gaps between the leaves and gaps between plants. But too much plant cover is also harmful, since many of the leaves will be in dense shade and so will be operating very inefficiently (Fig. 1.3).

The relevance of leaf area index (LAI) is shown by the example of rice. Of the two main types of rice, the original South Asian staple *(Orysa indica)* has a tall and leafy form of growth, with many side-shoots produced early on in the plant's life. It is well adapted to conditions of low fertility and deep flooding, but because of this the plant has an above-optimal LAI. The original Japanese variety *(Orysa japonica)*, on the other hand, is typically short and sturdy, less leafy, and with fewer side-shoots. The type of growth of this species gives rise to a more efficient canopy (optimal LAI), and the plant also responds well to nitrogen fertiliser.

Plant breeders have recently produced hybrid forms of rice which will, they hope, combine the good foliage characteristics and fertiliser responsiveness of *O. japonica* with the tropical adaptation of the *O. indica* varieties. As we shall see in Chapter 6, this 'Green Revolution' in rice cultivation has also had some undesirable side-effects.

The efficiency of photosynthesis

Less than half of the total solar radiation that is received on the earth's surface is in the visible spectrum that is suitable for photosynthesis. Of the remainder, on clear days about 45% of total radiation is infra-red and

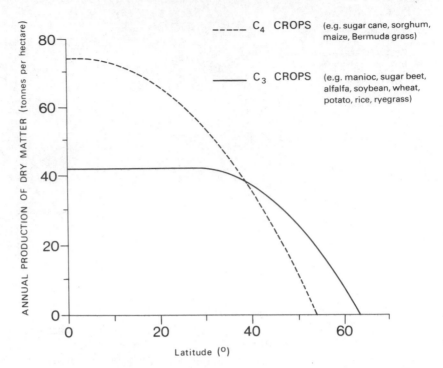

Fig. 1.4 Maximum recorded yields in different latitudes of C_3 and C_4 crops (after Cooper 1975).

about 10% ultra-violet, but both these are much reduced when there is any cloud cover.

Different types of vegetation vary somewhat in the proportion of this visible light that they can convert into carbohydrate through photosynthesis. Variations in LAI, differences in water and nutrient supply, and differences in environmental temperature will usually account for most observed differences in crop performance, but even if all these conditions are identical and optimal, there nevertheless remain certain inherent differences in photosynthetic efficiency between species. These differences in biological capability relate to two different ways of using carbon dioxide, the so-called C_3-pathway and the C_4-pathway. The C_4-pathway has been found to be quite common in species of tropical and/or arid origins (especially grasses), whereas the C_3-pathway is usual in temperate species.

Man's cultivated plants derive from both groups, and the maximum possible yields that have been recorded for each group in different latitudes suggest an interesting pattern (Fig. 1.4). The C_4 species, which include maize, sugar cane, sorghum and fodder grasses like Bermuda grass and Napier grass, seem to excel in tropical and subtropical regions. Over short periods, at least, such crops will convert up to 3–5% of the light energy they receive into the chemical energy of plant growth, which is a higher proportion than the C_3 species generally achieve in low latitudes.

One reason for this high efficiency is that the C_4 species can cope with very high light intensities during the middle of the day. The upright growth of a crop like sugar cane means that a narrow angle is maintained between the leaves and the sun's rays, so that the light intensity tends not to exceed the saturation point of the leaf. Maximum yields of C_3 species, for example rice, oil palm and manioc, are generally less impressive in the tropics. (Actual yields are, of course, usually much lower than those shown in Fig. 1.4, since only on experimental farms can all the factors of cultivation be kept optimal.)

As one proceeds to higher latitudes, the C_3 species begin to come into their own. Of the C_4 species, maize is in fact the only one which performs well at latitudes higher than 40°, and even here its best performancce cannot compare with that of crops like wheat and sugar beet. During the period of growth, these C_3 species typically convert up to 3% of light energy into plant growth, but of course only a proportion of this total production is available to man as food. In cereals about 50% of the total dry matter produced by the plant is actually grain, the remainder consisting of roots, stems and leaves which cannot be eaten.

The effect of temperature on crop performance

Apart from solar radiation, and the efficiency with which it is intercepted and photosynthesised by vegetation, there are also three other major ecological constraints on plant growth: unsuitable temperatures, moisture stress, and nutrient deficiency.

Temperature becomes important only at its extremes. Curves could be drawn similar to that for LAI in Fig. 1.3, indicating for each particular crop its diminished rate of growth in temperatures colder or hotter than a certain optimum range. For example, the cereals of temperate regions (oats, rye, wheat and barley) will produce some growth at comparatively low temperatures until a critical minimum is reached, between 0 °C and 5 °C. The optimum for these crops is between 25 and 31 °C, which represents the kind of weather experienced in England on hot summer days. The maximum for growth is around 37 °C, a level seldom reached in northern Europe but quite frequent in Mediterranean and subtropical climates.

Many tropical plants, on the other hand, are killed altogether if the temperature falls below 10 °C. Melons and sorghum, for example, have minimum temperatures for growth of 15–18 °C, optima from 31 to 37 °C, and maxima as high as 44–50 °C. The tropical grasses, such as maize and sugar cane, can tolerate even hotter conditions, and in sunlight they continue to photosynthesise up to 55 °C, provided that sufficient water and nutrients are available.

Studies of the primary production in natural ecosystems have shown that vegetation roughly doubles its productivity with every 10 °C increase in temperature, within the range − 10 to 20 °C mean annual temperature. A major reason for this correlation is that a low mean annual temperature usually occurs with a shorter growing season: in temperate latitudes, for example, the winter months have frequent suboptimal temperatures, occasional lethal frosts, and in any case less solar radiation is being received. Thus, although it is possible to correlate average temperature with productivity of vegetation on a global basis, this correlation is misleading since there is no direct cause–effect relationship.

As a general rule, agriculturalists reckon that provided the mean temperature of a given month exceeds 6 °C, then conditions will usually be adequate for the growth of some kind of crop. Livestock can also be maintained at this temperature without too many problems. On the basis of this assumption, the *thermal growing season* can be computed, which is simply the total number of 'warm' months, as defined above. Data

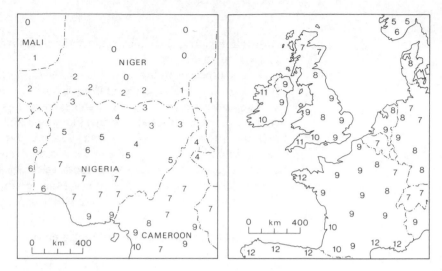

Fig. 1.5 Hydrological growing season in West Africa and thermal growing seasons in Western Europe (in months).

from meteorological stations in Western Europe show that the length of the thermal growing season varies from 5 months in Norway to 12 months on the north coast of Spain and in southern France (Fig. 1.5). In Norway the only crops possible in the short growing season are hardy varieties of barley, potatoes and hay. Forestry and permanent pasture are much more important to the farmer than his crops. As we move south the range of options open to the farmer increases, until in southern France two crops of rice per year can be obtained (with irrigation), and a number of subtropical plants will grow if protected in the winter.

Rainfall, evapotranspiration and soil moisture

If the transect envisaged above were to be continued into North Africa, then the thermal growing season would remain at the full 12 months right through into the tropics, except perhaps on mountains. Moreover, the lack of cloud, especially in the summer, means that areas like North Africa receive large amounts of solar radiation. Nevertheless, farming in this zone is normally confined to winter wheat and a few vegetable crops, and much of the land is used only for extensive grazing. The reason is obviously the lack of soil moisture during the hottest and sunniest time of the year, apart from isolated cases where irrigation is feasible. As we move from temperate to subtropical latitudes, temperature is replaced by rainfall as the dominant ecological constraint on agriculture.

Calculating the amount of rainfall that is needed per month for continuous plant growth is not at all straightforward, since so much depends on the demands of the crop, the amount of evaporated water that the rainfall must replace, the texture of the soil, and the characteristics of the rainfall itself. Both the intensity and the spacing of rainstorms is important: if all of a month's rain fell on one day, then drought would be almost inevitable at some later stage however adequate the monthly total appeared to be in aggregate terms, since much of the rain would have been lost as run-off. Conversely, very light falls of rain are also of limited use to vegetation, since most of the water is intercepted by the canopy and so fails to infiltrate into the soil. On a daily basis, 5 mm of rain is sometimes taken as the threshold of effectiveness in the tropics: less than this amount will seldom contribute anything to soil water reserves, unless it all falls in just a few minutes of concentrated downpour.

Various procedures are available for calculating whether or not a particular climate will cause drought problems for agriculture. Of these, Thornthwaite's *potential evapotranspiration* (PEP) index is perhaps the best known: if the actual evaporation of water at a site is found to exceed that which would potentially be lost from a vegetated surface if the soil were always moist (i.e., PEP), then we can assume that the rainfall is more than sufficient.

The calculation procedure is rather complex, however, and for less precise purposes an approximate rule of thumb is equally useful. In the tropics, it is often the case that a monthly rainfall of 100 mm (4 inches) will represent a total which is likely to be just sufficient for sustained crop growth. More conservatively, 125 mm (5 inches) has been suggested as an alternative. Similarly, in temperate regions 75 mm (3 inches) is sometimes used to indicate an approximately adequate monthly rainfall. On this basis *hydrological growing seasons* can be computed, which show how many months are likely to be suitable for crop growth in the absence of irrigation. In West Africa, using the 100 mm threshold, we find that the hydrological growing season declines from 9–10 months on the coast to 3–4 months in northern Nigeria, and 0–2 months on the edge of the Sahara (Fig. 1.5).

As in the European example above, the farmers in West Africa are restricted in their activities by the length of this growing season. Unless there is scope for irrigation during dry months, or unless non-agricultural activities can provide another source of income, then the dry season is likely to be a difficult period, especially towards the end when food supplies from the previous harvest are beginning to run out. In the highly seasonal climates of the Sahel region (e.g. around Kano), much of the population prefers the greater security of pastoralism as its chief source of livelihood. Some of the farming population, especially landless workers, have to migrate southwards in the dry season to try to find temporary jobs, working for the owners of plantations of tree crops (e.g. cocoa, oil palm), or employed in the towns. Both pastoralism and seasonal migration can be seen as adaptations to acute rainfall seasonality, but when a dry season is prolonged by unusual climatic conditions then even these adaptations fail to prevent disaster, as was shown by the Sahel famines of 1973–4 and 1985–6.

Replacing lost nutrients in the soil

Only 5–10% of a plant's dry weight consists of minerals derived from the soil, but these *nutrients* are absolutely crucial for the plant's healthy growth. The most important are: nitrogen, phosphorus, potassium, calcium, and magnesium. Nutrient deficiency is the fourth category of ecological constraint on agricultural production, and in one sense it is the most important. The constraints of solar radiation, temperature and rainfall are beyond the farmer's direct control: he usually adapts to these features of the environment, and he views each as a renewable resource more than as a force which he can substantially alter. Soil nutrients, on the other hand, are not self-renewing in the same inevitable way.

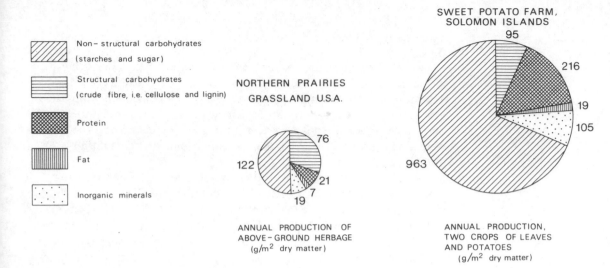

Non – structural carbohydrates (starches and sugar)

Structural carbohydrates (crude fibre, i.e. cellulose and lignin)

Protein

Fat

Inorganic minerals

NORTHERN PRAIRIES GRASSLAND U.S.A.

76
122
21
7
19

ANNUAL PRODUCTION OF ABOVE – GROUND HERBAGE (g/m² dry matter)

SWEET POTATO FARM, SOLOMON ISLANDS

95
216
19
105
963

ANNUAL PRODUCTION, TWO CROPS OF LEAVES AND POTATOES (g/m² dry matter)

Fig. 1.6 Quantities of net primary production, in various biochemical categories, for two vegetation types.

As examples of the rate of loss of soil nutrients, we can compare the chemical composition of the annual production of two kinds of vegetation, one natural and the other agricultural. The first is temperate grassland in the northern prairies of the U.S.A. (45 °N.), while the second is sweet potato fields in the tropical Solomon Islands (9 °S.) (Fig. 1.6). The total primary production of the two vegetation types is very different: on the prairies 245 g per m² of dry matter in the form of grass, but in the Solomons 1398 g per m² in sweet potato tubers and leaves. The total inorganic content in this production is also very different (19 g/m² and 105 g/m² respectively), but on the other hand as a proportion of total dry matter the mineral content is virtually identical: in each case 7.5% of primary production is in this category.

However, the most important contrast between the two ecosystems is in the way minerals are reused. In the prairie grassland, as in all natural ecosystems, the uptake of soil nutrients does not represent plant foods that are irrevocably lost to the system. In the winter the previous summer's growth of herbage dies back, and the nutrients are returned to the soil through decomposition of the dead plant litter by bacteria and fungi. Even if the grasses are removed by animal grazing, the nutrients will mostly be returned in the form of manure (but more patchily distributed!). This continual recycling of nutrients in natural vegetation means that any small losses of soil nutrients through leaching or run-off will be easily balanced by new rock weathering or by inputs of material in rainfall. The ecosystem thus achieves a balance between gains and losses.

In any agricultural system, however, this is not the case. Not only does the tilling of the soil and the creation of bare surfaces lead to the acceleration of losses through leaching and run-off, but also the crops removed from the land interrupt the natural recycling of nutrients. In the case of sweet potato cultivation (Fig. 1.6), at least 105 g per m² of soil nutrients are removed in the leaves, stems and tubers of the crop, and with the heavy tropical rainfall of the Solomon Islands losses through leaching are also likely to be substantial. As a result, sustained cultivation of the same piece of land is not possible unless the farmer makes some effort to replace lost nutrients, either by manuring, or by mulching (i.e. bringing in leafy material from surrounding areas), or alternatively by the purchase of artificial fertilisers.

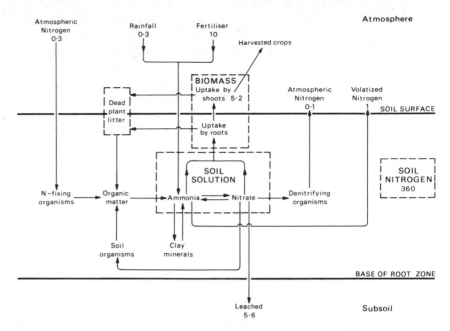

Fig. 1.7 The nitrogen cycle at Rothamsted, Hertfordshire, England, for the top 22 cm of a cultivated field. Quantities are in grams of nitrogen per m².

The nitrogen cycle

The three principal plant nutrients are N (nitrogen), P (phosphorus), and K (potassium). Of these, nitrogen is usually the most important agricultural fertiliser, in the form of ammonia (NH_4+). Ammonia is fairly rapidly broken down into nitrate (NO_3-) by soil bacteria. The chief natural source of ammonia in the soil is from the decomposition of organic matter, which itself derives from nitrogen-fixing soil organisms such as those associated with leguminous plants (e.g. beans, peas, clover), and secondly from the decay of the dead leaves, stems and roots of plants.

Nitrogen is taken up by plants in both ammonia and nitrate forms, being absorbed from the soil solution by roots. In agricultural systems this uptake by plants—which are then harvested and removed—constitutes one of the major losses of nitrogen that the farmer must replace. The second major loss is of dissolved nitrate which is leached out of the rooting zone by percolating rainfall. In the case of loamy soils in Hertfordshire, England (Fig. 1.7), research has shown that uptake by plant shoots averages 5.2 g of nitrogen per m², and leaching losses average 5.6 g per m². There are other losses from the breakdown of nitrate and ammonia into gaseous form, but by comparison these are of small importance, and are largely compensated for by small gains derived from rainfall and the activities of N-fixing organisms. It is worth noting from Fig. 1.6 that only about half to three-quarters of the nitrogen added as fertiliser is recovered in the crop, and that the crop itself removes only about 1% of the nitrogen present in the soil, most of which is unavailable until fixed by bacteria.

These figures indicate average rates of nitrogen flux, but there can be considerable variations from year to year and between different forms of land use. Leaching losses clearly depend on rainfall amount and intensity, which can vary considerably. Similarly, although N-fixation by soil organisms will result in small gains to the soil under any land use, the *Rhizobia* bacteria associated with legumes (e.g. peas, beans, clover, lucerne) can add up to 10 g per m^2 per year—in other words, they can add as much as the farmer does through artificial means.

Traditional *crop rotations* developed in Europe usually included one of these leguminous crops, for example beans, lucerne as a fodder crop, or clover sown with grasses. The Norfolk Four Course rotation of eighteenth-century England was as follows:

Year 1   Clover
Year 2   Wheat
Year 3   Turnips
Year 4   Barley

Both the clover and the turnips were grazed by sheep or other livestock, so that manure was also added to the soil. Rotations such as this enabled the farmer to achieve continuous use of the soil without recourse to fallowing. Yields were rather low by modern standards, but at the same time the agricultural inputs were small and were derived almost entirely from local sources of energy and nutrients.

The industrialisation of agriculture in developed countries proceeded very rapidly in the 1950s and 1960s, which were the years of cheap oil, economic growth and rising affluence. In the UK fertiliser has replaced crop rotations on most farms as the principal means of maintaining soil nutrient levels. Unfortunately, however, fertiliser is an energy-intensive product: each tonne of N applied to the soil has an energy requirement of about 1.8 tonnes of oil equivalent. As a result, the artificial means adopted to maintain the nitrogen cycle (and other nutrient cycles) in modern agriculture has been a major factor in the rising energy consumption of industrialised farming systems.

In the chapters that follow several different agricultural systems are compared, with attention being focused on the various kinds of energy input that are needed in order to overcome the different ecological constraints discussed in this chapter. For convenience, the agricultural systems are subdivided into *pre-industrial, semi-industrial* and *full industrial*, according to the degree of dependence on external energy sources and external markets. Historically, the transition from pre-industrial to full industrial has been regarded as inevitable and wholly desirable, but if some experts are right about an approaching energy crisis, then this assumption may need to be questioned. A study of food-producing systems that are not dependent on large energy subsidies could become vitally important for us in the industrialised countries, since for us a genuine energy crisis would also become a food production crisis.

2 Social pressures and decision-making in agrarian societies

Ecological versus social pressures

Before we embark on the seven case studies, which represent seven main types of agricultural system, it is worth considering how these particular case studies relate to each other. We have seen in the previous chapter that the main ecological constraints of solar radiation, crop type and cover, rainfall, and soil nutrient availability are likely to be found in a whole range of different permutations. For this reason alone, a strictly ecological perspective does not provide us with a very coherent framework for organising our thoughts about agricultural geography.

Some of the ecological pressures are rigid constraints in the sense that the farmer is virtually helpless to modify them. In other cases his response can be more positive. He can choose more suitable crops, or develop methods of cultivation which improve yields. The land can be irrigated, mulched, manured or rotated, or soils can be improved through artificial means. The farmer can supplement his (or her) own manpower through horsepower, from either animals or machines, or by employing other people's manpower through various means. The exact nature of the response does not depend on the environment, but rather on the society in which the farmer finds himself.

In this chapter I will discuss four ways in which a society can influence the decisions that farmers make. The influence operates through (a) population pressure, (b) technological innovation, (c) structures of social organisation, and (d) the values that farmers conform to when making decisions. Together, these social factors will help us to organise in our minds the reasons underlying the bewildering variety of agricultural practices that are encountered in the real world, and will put into context the seven case studies which follow in subsequent chapters.

Population pressure

The effect of population growth can be seen most clearly in the case of agrarian societies not much involved in selling their produce, and so not dominated by profit-making motives. Such societies are often pre-industrial in technology, and so are faced with the recurrent problem of replenishing the soil nutrients that are lost in the harvested crops, through soil erosion, etc. The appropriate solution to this problem will vary according to the degree of land shortage (Fig. 2.1).

If land is plentiful and there is no intention to maximise production, then the easiest course of action for the farmer is not to attempt the permanent cultivation of his fields through either a laborious or an expensive replacement of lost soil nutrients, but instead to leave the land for a while as fallow. A natural process of recovery will then replenish soil nutrients without any intervention by the farmer. A fallow period of more

Fig. 2.1 Extensive shifting cultivation, with forest fallow: the population density is under 10 per km², and the land reverts to secondary forest after only one year of cropping. The main crop is taro (*Colocasia esculenta*). (Bimin Valley, New Guinea Highlands).

than a year implies that the farmer's activities must shift from one piece of land to another, a process often termed *shifting cultivation*.

In the tropics fallow periods of up to 3–4 years are known as *grass fallows*, since little more than grasses and weeds will invade the abandoned fields during this period. A *bush fallow* implies that 5–8 years must elapse before cultivation occurs again, and in this case small shrubs and saplings will need to be removed before the crops can be planted. On the other hand, as a result of the longer period of recovery the fertility of the soil should be substantially improved. *Forest fallows* occur when periods of about 10 years or more elapse between short periods of cultivation. In temperate latitudes the same sequence can be identified, but the process of forest regeneration is more delayed.

The Danish economist Ester Boserup has investigated the amount of labour that is required in order to produce crops under these various systems of fallow. She finds that in Africa forest fallows require the least amount of work per unit of food produced, despite the initial effort involved in forest clearance, since the soil produced by burning the cleared vegetation is relatively fertile and free from weeds. Bush fallows and, in particular, grass fallows require as much or more labour in order to prepare the land, and crop yields tend to be lower. Permanent cultivation is the most laborious of all, since large inputs of labour are needed in mulching and weeding, and the yields may not be at all impressive. Data from other parts of the tropical world, such as New Guinea, would seem to support these ideas (Fig. 2.2).

In the light of these findings, Boserup claims that an increase in the intensity of cultivation will not take place in pre-industrial societies unless there is population pressure. Unless the farmer wants to produce a surplus over and above his subsistence requirements, and unless he is prepared to work harder for it, then there is no incentive for him to replace shifting cultivation by more intensive methods of land use. The change involves more work for the labour force, and so will be resisted. An increase in population, on the other hand, will mean that the luxury of long fallows can no longer be afforded. The land must be cultivated more and more

Fig. 2.2 Intensive shifting cultivation, with grassland fallow: the population density is about 100 per km^2, and the land is cultivated for up to 10 years before reverting to swamp grassland (Upper Kaugel Valley, New Guinea Highlands).

frequently in order to feed the growing numbers, and as a result new skills and larger work units will be needed.

In societies dependent largely on hand labour, the 'cost' of replacing soil nutrients therefore depends partly on the prevailing man : land ratio. In addition, however, there are inherent variations in the fertility of the soil. Even from land that appears to be highly infertile some crops can usually be obtained, but only at the cost of a substantial investment of labour in soil tillage and the application of manure, mulch or lime. During the early fourteenth century in England there was a period of sustained population growth, and in many places infertile, acidic soils were brought into cultivation through the application of such techniques. After the catastrophic mortality in the Black Death (1349) and other subsequent epidemics, much of this marginal land was abandoned: the effort required to overcome the soil nutrient deficiencies no longer seemed worthwhile when the same effort applied to other land would yield much better results.

The diffusion of innovations

Since the Industrial Revolution fertilisers have become increasingly available as a replacement for 'organic' techniques such as manuring. These innovations have helped to reduce the labour force needed to maintain agricultural systems, but at the same time they involve a dependence on external forms of energy. As we have seen, inorganic fertiliser can only be produced by means of industrial processes which rely heavily on electrical power, which itself derives mainly from fossil fuels. The most important fossil fuel in industry is oil, which at present rates of consumption is likely to be in short supply by the end of the century.

Fertiliser is only one of a number of industrial products which have been used to reduce the subservience of farmers to the problems posed by nature. We can divide the inputs into any farming system into (a) human labour, applied directly to crops or indirectly to the maintenance of draft animals, and (b) the externally-derived inputs which subsidise that labour, such as machines and their power source, fertilisers, pesticides, etc. These are termed *energy subsidies* because they all require fossil fuel energy for their manufacture, marketing and distribution, and therefore involve society in an energy cost.

These technical innovations have arisen in particular industrialised societies at particular times. In the same way, earlier advances in technology are likely to have had particular geographical origins, for example cultivated wheats (Near East, 5,000–6,000 B.C.), windmills (Persia, 600 B.C.), and the heavy plough (central Europe, 500 A.D.). These inventions subsequently spread elsewhere, with places close at hand usually receiving the benefits of the innovation sooner than more remote ones. This process of *geographical diffusion* is one reason for variation in agricultural systems: at any point in time the diffusion pattern for any particular technology is likely, at the global scale, to be incomplete.

More often, however, technologies are known about but are not adopted because they are regarded as being inappropriate. We have already seen how population growth can alter circumstances to make innovations seem more appropriate. The reasons for non-adoption of a particular technology are rarely as straightforward as simple geographical isolation from points of origin.

An organising concept used in this book is the extent to which farmers have adopted the general technology of the Industrial Revolution, which is what is implied by the terms pre-industrial, semi-industrial and full industrial. The precise boundaries of these categories are arbitrary, and their definition depends upon a knowledge of the extent to which human labour is supplemented by the energy subsidies of fertiliser, machinery, etc. Pre-industrial farming systems are those where fossil fuel inputs are zero or very small, below 10% of the total energy input that derives from man's activities (i.e. excluding solar energy, horse power, etc.). Semi-industrial systems are where fossil-fuel-derived inputs comprise 10–95% of the total. In full industrial systems the human energy input is below 5%, and generally so small as to be almost negligible.

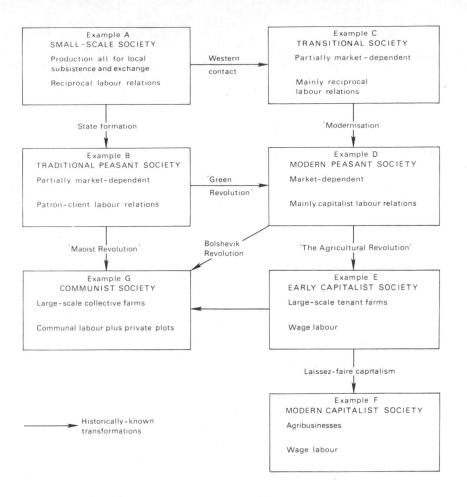

Fig. 2.3 Seven types of agrarian society, and their evolutionary relationships.

Seven examples of social organisation

The third general factor affecting farming decisions is the prevailing type of social organisation. Our seven case studies exemplify seven alternative paths in the evolution of society from the simplest of the pre-industrial forms to the most complex of those encountered in industrialised countries (Fig. 2.3). It would be wrong to see this process of social evolution as inevitable or unilinear, still less as being wholly desirable. The seven examples chosen as case studies to illustrate these various types are shown in Fig. 2.4.

Starting with Example A (a New Guinea village, Chapter 3), we have a subsistence system of shifting cultivators based entirely on pre-industrial technology. This type of agriculture is associated with a type of society which is increasingly uncommon in the modern world, but which arguably represents the starting-point for all agrarian societies. Like a few other places in the world isolated until recently from the mainstream of innovation diffusion, New Guinea still has examples of *small-scale societies*, virtually self-sufficient, and with production almost entirely for immediate consumption or local exchange, rather than for purposes of trade.

An enlargement in the scale of this sort of society, as a result of the growth in population and communications, led historically to its gradual transformation. The influence of trade became stronger, and encouraged the development of social stratification (lords and commoners, priests and

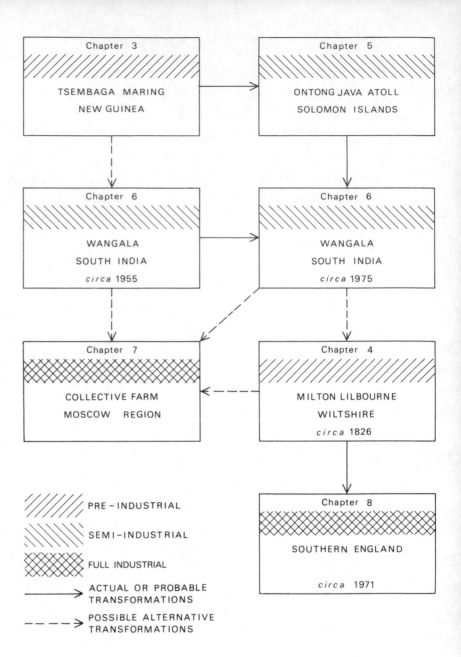

Fig. 2.4 Seven case studies of agricultural systems.

slaves, Brahmins and Untouchables). Unlike small-scale societies, which tend to be rather egalitarian, these *traditional peasant societies* are stratified: the relationship between a farmer and those who work for him becomes acknowledged as an unequal one. The farmer is the patron, the farm labourer is his client, and in both cases status is inherited from generation to generation. Examples are the feudal system of medieval Europe and the caste system of India. In Example B (Chapter 6), a village in South India *circa* 1955 is described. It represents a peasant society typical of parts of the Third World as yet largely untouched by the Industrial Revolution, but producing a small food surplus for purposes of trade despite a high density of population.

The influence of modern capitalism impinges rather differently on these two sorts of society. Small-scale subsistence societies have, in the face of 'western contact', become *transitional societies* with externally-oriented cash sectors coexisting with the traditional, subsistence-based society (see Example C, Ontong Java atoll, Chapter 5). Further modernisation of such societies leads to changes similar to those accomplished by the Green Revolution in more 'feudal' societies: the creation of a market-dependent society of peasant farmers employing wage labour and some industrial technology. There is an increased polarisation between rich peasants and landless labourers (see Example D, South India *circa* 1975, Chapter 6). Such *modern peasant societies* are very characteristic of rural areas in much of the Third World today.

The Industrial Revolution and accompanying social changes led to the emergence of two divergent types of modern farming system. In predominantly *capitalist societies* the engrossment of peasant holdings resulted in the formation of large-scale capitalist farms, which until the twentieth century were run with a largely pre-industrial technology (see Example E, Wiltshire *circa* 1826, Chapter 4). In recent decades such farms have had their manpower and horse power increasingly supplemented and replaced by industrial technology (see Example F, Southern England *circa* 1971, Chapter 8).

Elsewhere, however, there were peasant economies that were transformed into a very different mode of production from that found in England. In Russia and parts of Eastern Europe, collectivisation was imposed by *communist regimes*, producing agricultural systems like Example G, a collective farm in Moscow Region (see Chapter 7). This final type represents an alternative path of evolution from that which has occurred in societies subject to free market forces.

Social values and farmers' goals

The approach adopted in presenting these case studies is deliberately small-scale. As suggested above, they do represent general types of agricultural enterprise, but in themselves the studies described cover a few hundred people and rather limited tracts of land. One reason for this focus on the micro-scale is that only at this scale can we find sufficiently detailed information to make precise estimates of the magnitude of the various energy inputs and outputs.

Another important reason is that our explanations for agricultural geography must take into account the social values of individuals and their aspirations, or goals. The ecological problems that face farmers (e.g. drought, soil degradation) mean that to some extent they must adapt to the environment, but at the same time there will be many alternative adaptations that are equally effective from an ecological point of view (e.g. dry farming or irrigation, shifting cultivation or manuring). Ultimately, our explanations depend on how well we understand why certain decisions have been made by particular farmers, and this in turn demands a micro-scale focus. Such an understanding of decision-making becomes very difficult if we attempt to make generalisations at the scale of, say, the American Corn Belt or Monsoon Asia.

Farmers' decisions cannot be interpreted as if they were dictated solely by economic considerations. Of course, decisions which are economically disastrous (for instance, choosing to grow a crop climatically unsuited to an area) will not have any lasting effect on land use, but even amongst those alternatives which are feasible it is difficult, for practical reasons, for a person to make a fully 'rational' choice which will always turn out to be the most 'economic'.

Instead, we must view the farmer's decision-making as taking place within a framework of bounded rationality, since the capacity of any farmer to be fully informed and completely rational in organising his activities must be limited. Whether or not he actually desires to conform to the model of Rational Economic Man must also be in doubt, for it is clear that farmers (and other decision-makers) do not operate solely in order to maximise their income, or their security, or their leisure, or any other solely 'economic' benefit. It seems more realistic to view the farmer as someone who attempts to balance these and other, often conflicting, goals to achieve a satisfactory level of income, security, leisure, etc., rather than trying (and inevitably failing) to maximise for any particular aim.

We can, perhaps, envisage the farmer's goals as being motivated in three rather different ways:

1 He will aim to achieve physical well-being: he must satisfactorily provide for the present and future needs of himself and his dependents, either through food production or through earning a cash income or by a combination of the two, but at the same time must safeguard a certain amount of leisure time.
2 He will aim to achieve social recognition, by gaining status, respect and influence within the community in which he lives.
3 He will conform to some kind of ideology, which includes a belief in religion. Ideologies closest to our own are the hardest to recognise, but everyone has personal notions of what is right and wrong which influence his behaviour, as well as behaviour being influenced by more conscious 'economic' and 'social' objectives.

The prevailing state of land shortage, the technology at his disposal, and the social structure in which he operates will all pressurise the farmer to put more or less emphasis on each of these three groups of motives. Farming, like life, is a compromise between conflicting objectives, and the precise compromise that an individual adopts may represent a decision almost too complex to be fully rationalised even by the individual concerned.

3 Pre-industrial systems 1: New Guinea

New Guinea agriculture: Stone Age survival?

It has been estimated that of the 80,000,000,000 people who have ever lived on earth since the emergence of the species *Homo sapiens*, over 90% have lived as hunters and gatherers. Indeed, during over 99% of the period of his occupation of the planet, man made virtually no use of domesticated plants and animals, which first appear in the archaeological record a mere 10,000 years ago. This means that about 6% of the human population that have ever lived have been agricultural, and perhaps 3% have lived in industrial societies.

In starting our case studies with an agrarian society in New Guinea we are therefore a long way beyond the starting-point of man's food-producing activities. New Guinea is a large island north of Australia (see Fig. 5.1) and it is often thought of as the last outpost of the Stone Age. In the narrow, technological sense this is true (or was true until about 30 years ago). On the other hand New Guinea has a very long history of agriculture stretching back to around 9,000 years ago. At a time when Europe was still emerging from the last Ice Age, populated by small bands of nomadic hunters and gatherers, people in the New Guinea Highlands were already cultivating crops, digging canals to control the flow of water, and keeping herds of domesticated pigs.

The agricultural systems that emerged in New Guinea proved to be remarkably stable, and as a result of the isolation of this part of the world from the mainstream of agricultural innovations elsewhere, they were able to persist, with only small modifications, almost up to the present. The first major change in recent times was the adoption of the sweet potato, a root crop of South American origin which diffused into New Guinea in the seventeenth century via Indonesia. Coastal populations in New Guinea first came into direct contact with European traders in the nineteenth century, and as a result they soon became involved in the market economy. For them trade meant the acquisition of steel tools, in exchange for items of value to western commerce such as copra (dried coconut). Away from the coast, however, the mountainous interior remained completely unknown to the outside world until much later. This Highlands region was not explored by Europeans until the late 1930s, and its population was not properly under the control of the Australian administration until the late 1950s.

Living in the Highlands was a population of some 2 million subsistence farmers, cultivating taro and sweet potatoes at between 1,500 m and 2,500 m. The 'discovery' of these agricultural systems has therefore been extraordinarily recent, and although there has been rapid change in the last 30 years it is still possible to find systems of food production that are wholly pre-industrial in character. One such system is that of the Maring, an ethnolinguistic group of about 7,000 people living in the northern part of New Guinea. Maring agriculture was studied by an anthropologist,

Roy Rappaport, and by a geographer, William Clarke, in the early 1960s. Their research provides a fascinating case study of a pre-industrial mode of food production which is well adapted for fulfilling traditional subsistence needs in a tropical forest environment, but which in some ways is poorly adapted to the new cultural aspirations of New Guineans in the late twentieth century. The Maring case is typical of many rural societies in tropical countries which also have a traditional reliance on shifting cultivation (see Fig. 2.1).

The Maring environment

Rappaport's data on the Maring relate to the Tsembaga, a group of about 200 people. Their territory is mountainous, with most cultivation occurring on slopes of about 20°, but with substantial areas which are even steeper. Almost the entire area is covered with forest, which varies in type from lowland rain forest (between 700 and 1,200 m) through montane forests (1,200–1,800 m) right up to moss forest (1,800–2,100 m) (Fig. 3.1).

The soils in this area are generally poor, except close to the surface where there is a thin horizon enriched by organic matter derived from decaying forest litter. As might be expected with the very high rainfall (over 3,000 mm), this store of nutrients is quickly leached away when the forest cover is removed for agriculture, and as a result permanent cultivation would be difficult to maintain. Instead shifting cultivation is practised, and over the centuries this has to some extent altered the vegetation.

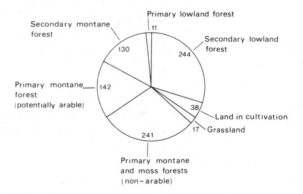

Fig. 3.1 Areas under different types of vegetation and land use within Tsembaga Maring clan territory, New Guinea (in hectares).

The Tsembaga Maring control a total area of 823 hectares, of which about 38 hectares are in cultivation at any one time. Of the lowland rain forests, only 11 ha are still primary, the rest having been converted into secondary forest through past cultivation. Some cultivated areas have been used too frequently, with the result that savanna grassland has become established (17 ha), dominated by the species *Imperata cylindrica*. This type of vegetation is resistant to reforestation, partly because it is quite frequently burnt by the Maring, either deliberately during hunting trips, or by accident. Most of the montane forest is primary or late secondary growth, but at least half of this land is much too steep and dissected ever to be used for agriculture. Similarly, all of the high-altitude moss forest is uncultivated, being too wet and cloudy, and its only economic value is for occasional hunting and collecting activities.

Fig. 3.2 A mixed vegetable garden in the New Guinea Highlands: traditional crops like sugar cane and *Hibiscus manihot* are interplanted with introduced crops like cabbages and onions (Bimin Valley).

Maring farming: exploitation or conservation?

In this environment quite protracted forest fallows are needed for the soils to recover after cultivation. At lower altitudes 15–25 years must usually elapse between periods of cultivation, but in the montane forest up to 35 years of fallow is needed. The period of cultivation is only 2 years, with 85–90% of the total yield occurring in the year which follows the fifth month after planting (Fig. 3.2).

The New Guinea forests are not at all rich in animal life nor in birds large enough to be hunted, and the rivers are too small to be of much importance for fishing. As a result, domestic pigs have an important role to play, providing in the diet protein and fat which would otherwise be in short supply. The main foods in New Guinea are all root crops which are rather deficient in protein: taro, sweet potatoes, yams and cassava, together with bananas, sugar cane and various other vegetables. These crops are grown together in plots that have been cleared of secondary forest and burnt, a process which gets rid of the litter and also releases the plant nutrients within it and makes them available for the crop. (Such plots are often called *swiddens*, an Old English word formerly used to describe the similar practices of Anglo–Saxon farmers.)

The diversity and structure of the New Guinea swidden in some ways mimics the characteristics of the forest itself, as Rappaport (1971) points out:

'As the crops mature the garden becomes more stratified and the plants make maximum use of surface area and of variations in vertical dimensions. This inter-planting discourages plant-specific insect pests. It allows advantage to be taken of slight variations in garden habitats, it is protective of the thin tropical soil, and it achieves a high photosynthetic efficiency.'

Other Maring land-use practices are equally conservationist in their effect: on steep slopes liable to slope-wash, simple erosion control is carried out by placing logs along the contour of the slope to retain the soil. The eventual regeneration of the forest after the abandonment of the swidden is also encouraged by the farmer, who removes useless weeds but often protects and encourages tree saplings which grow amongst his crops. This scrub eventually obliges him to abandon the plot, but on the other hand the forest succession is thereby safeguarded. If soil fertility were to be fully exhausted and the invading scrub discouraged, there would be a danger of *Imperata* grassland becoming established. This vegetation is much less effective in allowing the soil to recover its fertility, and because of its fire-resistant root system, it is a difficult kind of fallow vegetation to eliminate.

Clarke (1977) has argued that the stability of the Maring pattern of land use contains important lessons for 'advanced' societies intent on encouraging 'primitive' shifting cultivators to change their ways. In his view,

'The Maring have existed for centuries with stone-age habits and technologies; under the same conditions their survival could be projected far into the future, whereas the habits and technologies of the industrial world point to imminent collapse. It is an irony that while the Maring still live in a relatively stable ecosystem they are becoming so impressed and intrigued by the artifacts of the outside world's plundering economy.'

This theme is one I will return to later in the chapter, after a more detailed examination of the workings of the Maring economy.

Social organisation and settlement

As is usual in non-literate societies, it is impossible to state with confidence how long the Maring have been inhabiting the land that they now use. The people's own traditions suggest that they moved into the area about four generations ago, displacing another population that spoke a different language. The particular population studied by Rappaport, the Tsembaga Maring, consists of three major clans each of which owns one of the three subdivisions of the Tsembaga territory. Everyone has the right to hunt, trap and gather materials anywhere, but for agriculture a man is not supposed to use land outside his clan's territory.

The Tsembaga are not short of land, however. As Fig. 3.1 shows, the actual land in cultivation (38 ha) is only 9% of the total area that has ever been used, and in addition there is also primary rain forest that has not been touched for agriculture for many generations. Rappaport estimates that with very large pig herds, the Tsembaga's resources could support a population 40% larger than the actual numbers present in 1962 (the year of his research), assuming a minimum of 15 years' forest fallow.

Possibly as a result of this lack of population pressure, the rules governing land tenure are not rigidly adhered to. Members of one clan are not supposed to use land outside their own territory, but in fact land grants are often made from one clan to another. Similarly, a man claims ownership of each plot of land which he cultivates or has once cultivated, but if he is short of such sites he simply asks another member of his clan for a tract of land to be transferred to him for his use. Such requests are seldom refused, and this has the effect of preventing the emergence of social and economic inequalities between households or clans. It also protects the forest environment from being overexploited in some areas while others remain underused.

The Tsembaga, like most Maring groups, initially achieved control over their present territory through warfare. Some anthropologists have argued that warfare was one mechanism which limited population growth in New Guinea, particularly in cases where one clan had out-grown its land resources and no land grants were available from neighbouring groups. At present such fighting is not necessary for the Maring, and would in any case be forbidden by the government.

There is considerable cooperation between individuals in carrying out agricultural tasks. Men usually do the heavy work of cutting down trees, making fences to keep pigs out, and putting in soil retainers, whereas women do most of the work of weeding and harvesting. There is little variation between households in the amount of food produced, unless a family chooses to cultivate extra land in order to keep more pigs. Maintaining a large pig herd is, in fact, the only way of storing the energy of surplus root crops, which in themselves are very perishable. On the other hand the pig, once slaughtered, becomes an equally perishable product, and must be distributed and eaten without delay. The Tsembaga therefore tend to be a highly egalitarian society, with the burdens of work and the benefits of production shared equally amongst the population.

Maring houses are simple huts constructed out of forest timber and leaf thatch, and in the wet tropical climate they need to be rebuilt every few years. The temporary nature of housing allows the settlement pattern to change quite frequently, as sites of cultivation shift from one part of the territory to another. The terrain is rugged, and the root crops that are grown are both bulky and perishable. As a result, distance between place of residence and the swidden becomes an important factor. Each newly built house is likely to be sited within a tolerable distance of existing and future cultivation sites, especially when the household is maintaining a large pig herd. Pigs need to be fed each day with sweet potatoes, and they also need a good deal of supervision to prevent them from damaging the growing crops. The normal settlement pattern is therefore one of small clusters of houses and scattered homesteads.

Goals of the Maring farmer

The pattern of rural land use, and the structure of the agricultural systems that maintain this pattern, depend ultimately on the outcome of decisions made by individuals. As we saw in Chapter 2, such decisions can be envisaged as a compromise between (a) the desire to achieve physical well-being, and (b) the desire to achieve social recognition, but at the same time (c) they must not conflict with the person's social and religious ideology.

Among the Maring of New Guinea, all three objectives can be identified as motivating men and women in their agricultural activities. The need to satisfy strictly economic needs accounts for the majority of agricultural work and production, since sufficient land must be cleared, planted and cultivated to meet all of a family's basic food requirements. Dietary surveys show that on average each person consumes 2,952 MJ in food energy per year, mainly in the form of starchy root crops (taro, sweet potato, yams, banana). It is good ecological sense as well as nutritionally and socially desirable that the diet should include a variety of other vegetable foods, as well as supplementary animal protein. On the other hand as all of these products are perishable and, moreover, all are produced also by neighbouring populations, there is little purpose in growing a large surplus for storage or trade.

As in many other pre-industrial societies not threatened by population pressure or land shortage, the Maring household does not attempt to maximise its production of crops. The basic food-producing activities are important since they maintain life and provide leisure time, but a man's predominant interest is more likely to be in activities that in strictly economic terms appear to be wasteful or even destructive. These include long hours spent hunting small mammals and birds, often for little tangible reward; indulging in rituals associated with religion and warfare (or its prevention); and accumulating very large pig herds.

Pigs serve not as a steady source of meat in the diet, but rather as a means of achieving status through ownership and through conspicuous display during occasional large feasts, themselves events with religious significance. At the feasts the pig meat is distributed throughout the community and to neighbouring populations for immediate consumption, so that a man's 'wealth' appears to be rapidly dissipated—but with substantial rewards of a more intangible kind.

Women's interests centre on these same rituals and displays, and indeed it is their work in sweet potato production which enables the pig herds to be maintained. Women are also very much involved in caring for their children and families, although it must be said that less is known about what motivates women's behaviour in New Guinea, mainly because male anthropologists outnumber female ones!

With both men and women, therefore, achieving social recognition and reinforcing the Tsembaga Maring ideology are important motives influencing agricultural decision-making. They are difficult to separate, but in combination these social and ideological considerations result in many activities which are not explicable simply in terms of the achievement of physical well-being. This is a question of interpretation which we shall return to when considering the 'efficiency' of the Maring agricultural system.

European contact

Our information about the Maring comes from the detailed surveys of Roy Rappaport in the period 1962–3. At this time the Tsembaga had been exposed to the influence of the outside world to a very limited extent: the first patrol of the Australian administration crossed their territory in 1954, but the Government did not officially regard the area as controlled until 1962. In that year two young Tsembaga men had left the area to work as contract labourers, but they had not yet returned. The Tsembaga remained unmissionised, so that in most ways traditional life continued unchanged.

In two important respects indirect contact with the Western market economy had actually began much earlier, in the 1940s. During this period there were epidemics of measles and dysentery, again probably of European origin, which may have reduced somewhat the total population. Steel tools also began to arrive via traditional trade routes, so that stone tools had gone out of use completely by the early 1950s. Measurements made elsewhere in New Guinea comparing the performance of steel and stone axes show that the steel tool is about three times more efficient. In other words, the task of clearing trees and bushes now takes about one-third of the time that it used to. But in general the Maring in 1962 do seem to represent a truly pre-industrial system of agriculture.

Agricultural inputs

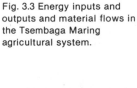

Fig. 3.3 Energy inputs and outputs and material flows in the Tsembaga Maring agricultural system.

In Fig. 3.3 the functioning of the Tsembaga Maring agricultural system is simplified to show only the principal inputs and outputs that are of human origin and significance. As in most pre-industrial systems that lack draft animals (horses, oxen, etc.), the predominant input is the

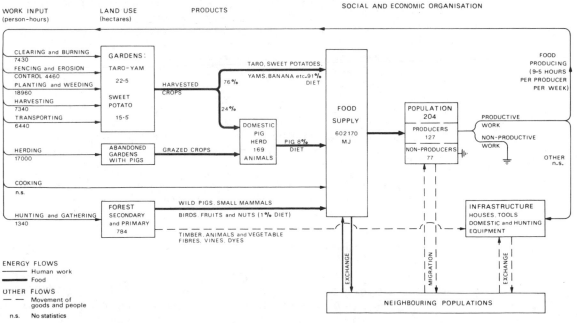

mechanical energy of human labour, shown in Fig. 3.3 in person-hours of work per year for the whole community. Out of the total population of 204 there are 127 potentially productive persons (i.e. those over 15 years of age). These persons work on average for 9.5 hours per week in food-producing activities, excluding the time needed to prepare and cook food.

Surveys elsewhere in the New Guinea Highlands by the anthropologist George Morren have shown that food preparation would probably add another six hours per week to the average adult's food-producing work, but even so the average work-load is clearly not heavy. On the other hand many of the so-called producers among the Tsembaga are too old to do much work or are nursing young children, so that some individuals' work inputs will be rather greater than the average.

There are few other inputs to agriculture. The Tsembaga produce almost all the commodities they need. There is some exchange of pigs with neighbouring groups, and some movement of population, especially of women who migrate in and out of the area when they get married. In practical terms, however, we can state that the Tsembaga Maring are a self-sufficient population whose food-producing system depends entirely upon rather modest energy inputs in the form of human work.

The procedure for converting the total work input into an energy equivalent is shown in Table 3.1. Rates of energy expenditure for different tasks vary considerably, with jobs like bush clearance by men requiring double the rate of energy expenditure that is needed for the rather sedentary tasks carried out by the women, such as weeding. Using these data, the total energy input into agriculture can be computed as 42,390 MJ per year for the whole community, a figure which becomes relevant when compared to the output of energy that the system generates.

Table 3.1 Procedure for calculating the energy input into Maring agriculture.

Activity	Work input (person-hours per year)	Rate of energy expenditure (MJ per hour)	Total input (MJ per year)
Clearing and burning	7,340	1.271	9,329
Fencing and erosion control	4,460	0.951	4,241
Planting and weeding	18,960	0.619	11,736
Harvesting	7,340	0.488	3,582
Transporting	6,440	0.876	5,641
Herding	17,000	0.397	6,749
Hunting and gathering	1,340	0.830	1,112
Agricultural system total	62,880		42,390

Source: work input: Rappaport 1968; rate of energy expenditure (adjusted for the sex ratio and body weight of the Tsembaga Maring): Norgan *et al.* 1974.

Agricultural outputs

The crops produced by the agricultural work are partly consumed directly by the Maring population, contributing an estimated 91% of the diet, and are partly fed to the pigs. There are two crops which provide heavy yields of food not much liked in the diet, namely sweet potatoes and cassava, and these are fed to the pigs. The size of the pig herds fluctuates according to the long-term religious cycle, the culmination of which is a series of feasts at which the pigs are slaughtered. This point arises when the work of cultivating enough land to feed the pigs becomes onerous. In 1962, when the pig herds were becoming excessive in their demands, 24% of the food energy produced was being fed directly to them, with more crops being fed indirectly by allowing the pigs to root about in abandoned gardens.

In the long term, about 8% of the diet derives from pig meat, but the figure is misleading in that consumption is so irregular. Pigs consumed in 1962 were derived from crops fed to them over the 3–4 preceding years, and apart from occasional wild pigs that are hunted, in some years many months elapse without pigs contributing at all to the diet.

Wild forest products are also shown in Fig. 3.3. Although not strictly 'agricultural' in the European sense, these are included as an integral part of the food-producing system. Their contribution to the diet is small in energy terms (about 1%), but as sources of variety in the diet, and as sources of fat and animal protein, they are quite important. Moreover, for house-building and the making of tools, fibres, vines and dyes from the forest are of vital importance.

The total supply of energy for consumption that the system generates can be estimated as follows:

1   Harvested crops: 721,000 MJ (gross output, of which 24% is fed to the pigs).
2   Hunted and collected items: 6,020 MJ.
3   Consumed pigs: 48,180 MJ.
    Total: 775,220 MJ per year,
    or 10.4 MJ per person per day.

By comparison, in the USA and Canada in 1979 the population dependent on agriculture (10 million people) produced just over 1,500 MJ per person per day in edible foodstuffs, about 150 times more. Almost all human societies will lie somewhere between these two populations in their gross energy productivity. New Guinea and North America thus provide end-points in the continuum which extends all the way from self-sufficient agricultural societies dependent on their own human energy resources to mass-consumption societies very heavily subsidised by exploiting the energy resources of fossil fuels.

Efficiency of the system

The 'efficiency' of any human enterprise can be assessed in a multitude of different ways, but in this book we shall consider four different measures of the performance of agricultural systems:

1   The *energy ratio:* the edible energy produced by the sysem in a net form (i.e. excluding animal fodder), divided by the total human-derived energy input (in this case, work).
2   The *gross energy productivity (GEP):* the total food energy produced by the system, in consumed and other forms, divided by the total population. This statistic thus shows the gross energy

production per person per year, from which the daily energy productivity can easily be derived.

3   The *surplus energy income:* the Maring do not produce any income in the monetary sense, but they do produce an energy surplus in the form of crops fed to pigs. For them, this represents the perceived income of surplus energy, and can be calculated in MJ per person per day.

4   The *energy yield,* in terms of net food output per hectare. In the case of shifting cultivation, the area required for fallow land must be included in the total exploited area.

For the Tsembaga Maring, we already have data for calculating these efficiency ratios from Fig. 3.3

The energy ratio for the system as a whole is 14.2, which implies that every unit of energy expended generates 14.2 units of net food production. The energy ratios of different subsystems of the economy can also be calculated:

Crop production:	20.9
Pig keeping:	3.2
Hunting and gathering:	5.4

The production of basic carbohydrates in the diet is by far the most efficient subsystem, yielding over 20 units of output per input unit. The minor contribution to the diet provided by the various foods which are hunted and collected in the forest is much less efficient, but least efficient of all is the keeping of pigs. Any intermediate step in a food chain inevitably diminishes the ultimate yield of energy, and in the Maring case the Energy Ratio of 3.2 for pigs shows why only a small proportion of their diet can derive from this source.

The food energy channelled towards pigs represents the only significant surplus that the Maring economy generates over and above that consumed in subsistence foods. As shown above, the GEP of the Maring averages 10.4 MJ per person per day, about 22% above the population's actual consumption of food energy. The surplus energy income, or pig food over and above subsistence, thus averages 2.3 MJ per person per day.

The fourth efficiency measure, the energy yield, is inevitably very low because of the large area that has to be maintained in forest fallow. The total usable area of 412 ha thus yields only 1,460 MJ per hectare in net food energy, which is very low by world standards. One agricultural hectare will only support two persons at the Maring standard of living.

Threats to stability

In the absence of external influences, there seems to be little doubt that the Maring agricultural system could persist for as long into the future as it has existed in the past. Population growth is the main threat to cropping systems based on shifting cultivation, since any tendency for the forest fallow period to be shortened can lead to the prevention of forest regeneration. In the New Guinea Highlands the existence of large tracts of *Imperata* grassland is widespread evidence that this problem has not always been successfully avoided. Such areas of man-made savanna tend to be self-perpetuating, since their most important use is for hunting which usually involves the use of fire.

In the area occupied by the Maring such grasslands are not at all extensive, but it is not clear whether this is evidence of a successful long-term adaptation to the environment, or whether instead it indicates a relatively brief history of occupation. Nevertheless, as it was managed in the 1960s Maring agriculture was notably conservationist in its intent: the forests and their soils were viewed as productive capital to be safeguarded for the future, not as resources to be exploited. As William Clarke (1977) suggests,

'They preserved for their children a habitat and set of resources only slightly modified from what they had inherited themselves, and they foresaw their children carrying on the same tradition.'

All this is now beginning to change. The reasons for the inexorable disappearance of the pre-industrial modes of food production of 'palaeotechnic' man are well summarised by Clarke (1977), referring again to the Maring of New Guinea:

'The pre-industrial world has its own set of debilitating and disabling diseases, its discomforts, its high infant mortality, its often far from ideal nutrition, its own kinds of environmental problems, and its comparatively limited opportunities. There is no reason why palaeotechnic man should hold to these in the face of neotechnic promises of a better life.'

For the New Guinea villager, the main ticket available for entry into this modern world is the production of *cash crops*. With Government encouragement, Highlanders have turned to a number of products which are in demand in local urban centres (pigs, vegetables) and in export markets (coffee, tea, pyrethrum). The prices received are not high, nor are they reliable, but the income generated is sufficient to enable villagers to acquire some of the benefits and novelties of the industrial world (Fig. 3.4).

Some of the results of the 'development' process are bizarre. A New Zealand sociologist, Ron Crocombe (1971), recalls a visit to a New Guinea village that grew coffee, producing just enough income to support a very small village shop. One of the few goods for sale was two-ounce tins of Nescafé costing $0.60 each.

'While drinking Nescafé with some men in the village, one of them asked me how much per *pound* it cost, and I said $4.80 a pound. "Why", he asked, "do we have to sell our coffee for 10 cents a pound?" '

Crocombe comments that although it could hardly be foreseen that part of the meagre coffee income of these villagers would be spent on buying Nescafé at 48 times the price per pound, the general result of 'development' is predictable. Under free market conditions there is every encouragement for farmers to abandon subsistence in order to make money, but it is not the consumers but the manufacturers and merchants who control the terms of trade and ways in which the money can be spent (see Chapters 5 and 6).

Ecological stability is threatened by the trend towards cash cropping for two reasons. One is that the new crops are much less familiar, not fitting well into traditional swidden cycles and often requiring inputs such as

Fig. 3.4 A New Guinea Highlander processing coffee beans: the metal and plastic containers that he is using are some of the imported goods that are most eagerly sought in the early stages of European contact (Tsak Valley).

fertiliser in order to yield productively. These crops may be cultivated with much less sensitivity to environmental degradation. The second reason is that villagers become dependent on only one or two favoured cash crops (e.g. coffee). The diversity and stability of the old polycultural cropping is replaced by a monoculture which is more liable both to natural and to economic hazards. For example, in 1986 coffee rust disease spread to New Guinea. The damage it causes will particularly affect those farmers now dependent on coffee as a cash crop.

The inherent stability of the Maring agricultural system has therefore been based on a long-term adaptation to an environment which is now rapidly changing. The tropical rain-forest environment remains the same, but the cultural environment in which the Maring now find themselves is one where numerous changes in agriculture are perceived as being necessary. As a result, the Maring agricultural system is being altered from the pre-industrial pattern to a semi-industrial one within the space of a single generation, with ecological side-effects which cannot yet be fully foreseen.

4 Pre-industrial systems 2 : Wiltshire in the 1820s

Pre-industrial farming in Britain

'The houses were, in general, from ten to twelve feet square; the walls were made of rough stone and mud, whited over and about nine feet high; no ceiling; rough rafters covered with old rotten black thatch; . . . the floor nothing but bare earth; no chimney, but a hole at one end of the roof to let out the smoke . . . The pig eats with the family, and generally sleeps in the same place. The potatoes are taken up and turned out into a shallow basket. The family squats round this basket and take out the potatoes with their hands; the pig stands and is helped by some one, and sometimes he eats out of the pot . . . The family sleep, huddled up together, on dead weeds or a little straw in one corner of the hole, and the pig on a bed in another corner' (Cobbett 1834).

These words might be taken as a description of a New Guinea village as seen through the rather shocked eyes of a European traveller. The few possessions, flimsy housing, dependence on root crops, and close relationship with domestic pigs, all suggest a simple pre-industrial farming economy not unlike that of the New Guinea Highlands (Chapter 3).

The description is, in fact, taken from a letter written by the radical journalist and farmer, William Cobbett, during his journey through Ireland in 1834. Cobbett saw amongst the Irish peasantry poverty and deprivation that was worse even than the situation at that time in rural England, and a standard of living certainly much lower than that of the Maring people discussed in the previous chapter.

The similarity between rural Ireland in the early nineteenth century and pre-contact New Guinea is, however, only superficial, as William Cobbett's description of the equally impoverished Irish farmers makes clear:

'The farmers . . . sell the corn to the corn-dealers, who send almost all of it to England. The farmer and his family are all in half-nakedness or rags; their lot is little better than the mere labourers. They raise wheat and barley and oats and butter and pork in great abundance, but never do they taste any of either, except, perchance, a small part of the meal of the oats. Potatoes are their sole food.'

Like those of New Guinea at the present day, Irish—and for that matter English—agricultural systems in the early nineteenth century were almost entirely pre-industrial in technology. For most of the agricultural population these systems provided levels of welfare that were no better than—and often inferior to—those of swidden cultivators in the modern Third World. On the other hand, the majority of British farmers 150 years ago were already part of a capitalist society, so that for most people in rural areas social and political factors (e.g. the pattern of land ownership, prices, wage levels, rents) had become the most important determinant of welfare, rather than 'technology' as such.

The situation in rural Britain in the early nineteenth century is therefore of interest since it provides an example of pre-industrial farming very different from New Guinea's in social organisation. Whereas societies like the Maring are highly egalitarian in living standards, and have very little division of labour other than that between the sexes, in Britain during the Industrial Revolution we see agriculture being organised so that the distribution of its benefits becomes increasingly unequal, with a growing difference between the respective roles of the land-owners, the farmers, and the farm labourers. The differentiation was geographical as well as social, as the Irish case shows, but in this chapter I shall focus on a single place without considering in detail its linkages with surrounding areas. The place chosen is in the chalklands of Wiltshire in Southern England, where the agricultural system was described in some detail by William Cobbett during one of his 'Rural Rides' in 1826.

From peasantry to landless labourers

In Wiltshire, as elsewhere in England, the period 1700–1800 was one of painful transition for the bulk of the agricultural population. In the late seventeenth century there still existed in much of rural England a largely peasant economy, founded on the rights of the peasant to cultivate land in the open fields and to graze his animals on the common. His largely subsistence economy was practised within a village society which provided 'social security' in many forms, and which shielded him from the market economy that was beginning to emerge in a starkly capitalist form in the towns and manufacturing districts.

By the early nineteenth century, visitors to England from the continent of Europe were surprised to find that the peasantry as a class no longer existed, except in more remote parts such as the Lake District, the Highlands of Scotland, and Ireland. In contrast with France and Italy, where small-scale peasant farming persisted right into the middle of the twentieth century, in England agriculture was no longer dominated by small-scale subsistence producers operating within a communal village system. Through the twin processes of *enclosure* and *engrossment* of holdings, the peasantry had been replaced by a class of landless agricultural workers, employed on a wage basis by farmers increasingly involved in the various 'improvements' that accompanied the Industrial Revolution.

These improvements involved the adoption of new crops, in particular fodder crops such as turnips which enabled herds of livestock to be kept over the winter. The new crops made possible new crop rotations, and the larger herds provided manure. Together, these two changes reduced the amount of fallow land, and so increased farm output. There were also improved breeds of animals and a few limited changes in farm tools and machinery (Fig. 4.1).

However, a pre-condition for the successful spread of this *Agricultural Revolution* was the removal of common rights to the open fields and the abolition of communal flocks and herds. With individual land tenure there also emerged the possibility for smallholdings to be easily amalgamated into larger and more 'efficient' farms. Moreover, the

This four Wheel Drill Plow, with a Seed and a Manure Hopper, was first Invented in the Year 1745. and is now in Use with W.ᵐ Ellis at Little Gaddesden near Hempstead in Hertfordshire. where any person may View the same. It is so light that a Man may Draw it. but Generally drawn by a pony or little Horse —

Fig. 4.1 New technology of the Agricultural Revolution in England: William Ellis's seed drill, one of the many similar innovations in the middle of the eighteenth century (from Ellis's *The Farmer's Instructor,* 2nd edn 1750).

peasants whose common rights had been swept away were now exposed to the full force of the market economy, and increasingly they formed a dependent class of agricultural workers available for employment by the farmers. In the depression years of low prices that followed the peace of 1815 many small farmers were forced to sell or rent their land and so join the ranks of the landless labourers, whose numbers were in any case being increased by steady population growth.

These, in outline, were the changes that had already occurred throughout Southern, Eastern and midland England by the 1820s. In the preceding half-century there had been another set of changes, those in the industrial sector, which were summarised as follows by William Cobbett (1826):

'There is something new in the manner and shape of manufacturing. Formerly the business was carried on in all parts of the country: now it has been so managed, the taxing and paper money system has created such a mass of monopolies, has drawn the wealth of the country into such great heaps, as to cause the manufacturing work-people to be collected into enormous masses, and that, too, in those parts of the country least productive of food.'

In response to this market, agriculture became increasingly commercial in its mode of operation. The turnpike roads and canals enabled counties like Wiltshire to send corn, sheep and wool to Bristol and London. A labour market also began to operate, and in a quite ruthless way. The landless poor were both too numerous and too disorganised to prevent themselves from being exploited for very low wages, and for many only the continued existence of Poor Laws prevented actual starvation. The smaller farmers themselves were being squeezed by low prices, inflation and taxation. While agricultural propagandists such as Arthur Young rejoiced at the 'amazing effects' wrought by the 'glorious spirit of improvement', most of the rural population of Britain viewed the workings of agriculture in the late pre-industrial period in a rather different light.

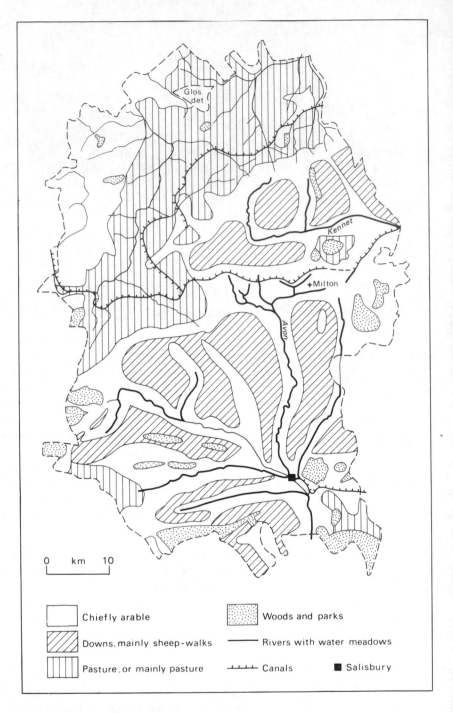

Fig. 4.2 Land use in Wiltshire, England *circa* 1800 (from Davis 1794).

Legend:
- ☐ Chiefly arable
- ▨ Downs, mainly sheep-walks
- ▥ Pasture, or mainly pasture
- ▨ (dotted) Woods and parks
- — Rivers with water meadows
- ┼┼┼┼ Canals
- ■ Salisbury

0   km   10

Map labels: Glos. det., Kennet, Milton, Avon

South Wiltshire in 1826

North and South Wiltshire are as different as chalk and cheese in the most literal sense (Fig. 4.2). The bare chalk hills and valleys of the south are a country of cereals ('corn') and sheep, in sharp contrast to the clay vales of the north which are still noted for pasture, dairy farming, and cheese making. Between the chalk escarpment and the softer rocks to the north is a belt of greensand, which has light soils suitable for most arable crops. By the 1820s both parts of the county were mainly enclosed, but the enclosure process had been much more recent in the chalk country.

The county was still almost wholly agricultural, apart from a small woollen textile industry in towns like Salisbury, Wilton, Bradford-on-Avon and Warminster.

Most of the parishes in the chalk country, and many of the large farms within these parishes, have had from earliest times a distinctively elongated shape. The parishes typically extend in strips from the chalk plateau down into one of the broad river valleys that dissect the hills, and they thus provide for their population access to a variety of resources. The river and its valley provide water and meadow land, the valley sides are good arable land, and the chalk downs provide pasture and woodland. The settlements are generally in the valleys, as near to the river as possible. By the end of the eighteenth century the use of water meadows, arable and downland pasture had become functionally interconnected, through a specialised sheep-and-corn economy which required access to all three types of land. The problem for the small land-holders was that the steady erosion of the old communal rights to all three kinds of land meant that this tripartite form of rural economy was for them no longer viable. Increasingly, the smallholders were forced to sell or rent their land to larger land-holders, and to become labourers rather than independent farmers.

In South Wiltshire, as elsewhere, the period 1790–1830 was one of steady impoverishment for the labouring class, much to the anger of William Cobbett who witnessed its effects during his famous 'Rural Rides' in the 1820s. Of the Valley of the Avon, for example, he wrote 'the labourers here *look* as if they were half-starved'; houses and manors were falling down, as a result of 'the gradual decay in all except what apertains merely to *the land* as a thing of production for the distant market'. It was in this valley that he undertook a study of one particular parish, Milton Lilbourne, to discover exactly how much it produced, and how its agricultural production was distributed amongst its population. This classic piece of early analysis provides us with our detailed case study.

Milton Lilbourne parish

The parish of Milton Lilbourne is in the Vale of Pewsey, right at the headwaters of the River Avon (Fig. 4.3). The nearest market town is Devizes. The Kennet and Avon Canal, which was built in 1810 to link London with Bristol via Reading, actually runs through the parish, but Milton was nevertheless a fairly remote place in the 1820s. The parish is small, measuring only 9 km by 3 km, but it is typical of the region in that it extends in a strip across the Vale of Pewsey, encompassing areas of chalk grassland, arable fields on grassland, and water meadows in the valley (Fig. 4.4).

The population of the parish was on the increase during this period. In 1821 there were 632 persons recorded in the census, and by 1831 the total had risen to 660. As elsewhere in the region, enclosure of the open fields had taken place informally in the previous century, and the process was completed by means of parliamentary acts (for Milton, in 1791 and 1823). As a result of this process and that of engrossment, use of the land had become concentrated in a few hands. Information from tithe surveys made a few years later than 1826 shows that only 4 persons owned 68% of the agricultural land, whereas about 600 persons in the parish were

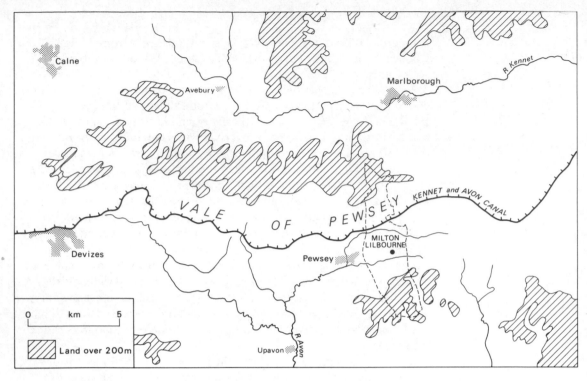

Fig. 4.3 Vale of Pewsey, Wiltshire, showing Milton Lilbourne parish.

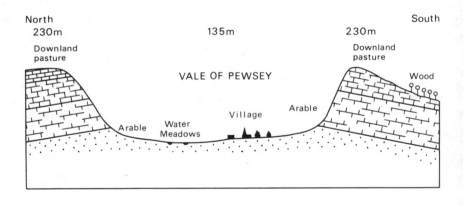

Fig. 4.4 Geology in cross-section, north to south, across Milton Lilbourne parish.

effectively landless (Table 4.1). The big owners were all absentee landlords, renting their farms to tenants. Even in terms of occupiers, however, the same picture emerges: 86% of the land was in the hands of 11 big farmers, with holdings of over 20 hectares each.

The land-use pattern is also recorded in the tithe surveys (Fig. 4.5), with arable farming clearly predominant. Arable occupies two-thirds of the total area of the parish, including the whole of the valley apart from water meadows, and most of the downland that was not too steep for ploughing or not too remote for manuring. Downland still under sheep

Table 4.1 Ownership of agricultural land in Milton Lilbourne.

Amount of land owned (ha)	Number of landed or landless people	Total area (ha)	(%)
Nil	About 600	0	0
Under 21	55	140	10
21–40	1	34	2
41–80	2	170	12
81–120	1	98	7
Over 120	4	949	68
Total	About 660	1,391	100
Non-agricultural land (roads, canals, built-up area)	—	61	—

Source: Wiltshire Tithe Apportionments, 1840.

Fig. 4.5 Areas under different types of vegetation and land use, Milton Lilbourne parish, 1840 (in hectares).

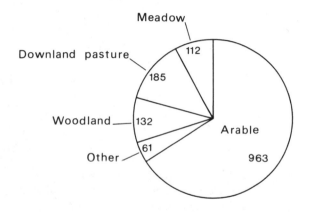

pasture is the second most important land use, followed by woodland and water meadow. All these three played vital subsidiary roles in the agricultural economy: the downland provided pasture for sheep, especially summer pasture at a time when the arable fields were all under crops; the water meadows supplied hay for winter feeding, and also a useful 'early bite' of grass for the sheep in spring; and the woodland was the source of coppice timber, used for numerous purposes including the hurdles used to make sheep folds.

The ecology of sheep-and-corn farming

We do not know exactly what crops were being grown on the arable land at Milton, but even in 1826 probably very little would have been fallow. The most valuable crops in this region were wheat and barley, but in order to prepare the soil for these crops its nutrient status had to be improved by means of manuring. To ensure a supply of manure was the principal reason for keeping a flock of sheep.

The sheep's mobility was one important means of achieving large-scale transfers of manure for little human effort, and over terrain far too steep

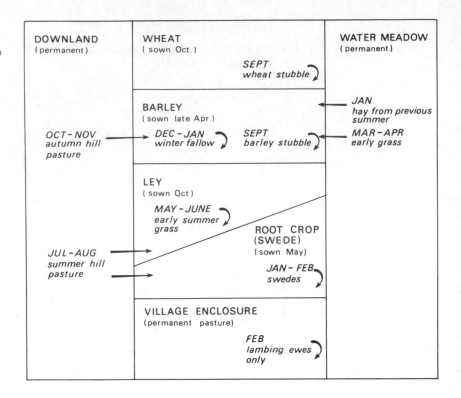

Fig. 4.6 Role of sheep in the sheep-and-corn economy, showing where grazing occurs and where dung is deposited, by month.

SEPT   Sources of sheep food in different months

         Distribution of sheep dung, through folding

for horses and carts. Each morning the flock would walk 2–3 miles for its food, returning in the evening the same distance. Most of the dung would be dropped at night, when the sheep were crowded into folds on the arable land.

The sheep's adaptability in diet was also important. In the late eighteenth century fodder crops like turnips and swedes were increasingly adopted as a winter feed for sheep, and in Wiltshire irrigated water meadows were constructed in the valleys to provide early spring grass and hay. These changes (a) enabled more animals to be kept in the winter, thus dropping more manure actually on the fields where subsequent corn crops would be grown; and (b) enabled the better parts of the downland to be ploughed up for corn, since their role as pasture was much less crucial.

The relationship of land use to manure use is shown in Fig. 4.6. The land-use pattern of a typical large farm in an area like the Pewsey Vale is shown, simplified into three main categories:

1   *Downland pasture:* provided sheep food in the autumn and mid-summer periods, but most manure was transferred by the sheep to the arable land through nightly folding.

2   *Arable land:* a three-course rotation is shown, with (a) winter wheat, followed by (b) spring barley, followed by (c) either a grass ley (often rye grass or clover) or a root crop such as swedes. This third type of land then reverted to winter wheat in the following year.

3   *Water meadow:* sheep that grazed here in the early spring were usually folded on the former wheat stubble that was soon to be sown with barley. The meadows also produced a late summer crop of hay, which was a useful winter supplement for all the farm animals.

By means of this nicely integrated system of manure transfers and rotations, output could be greatly increased. On the better soils (e.g. the greensand of Pewsey Vale), two crops out of three were of cereals. On the downland, where soils were thinner, or on farms with inadequate sheep flocks, or in fields too remote for sheep folding to be feasible, less intensive rotations were practised. Even so, corn crops were generally being obtained for 50% of the time.

Sheep were also valuable for their wool, and since the flock could not be allowed to multiply indefinitely, surplus animals were sold off to be fattened elsewhere for the market. Animals other than sheep were unimportant under this farming regime. A few cows and pigs were kept for domestic purposes, and there was, of course, a great need for horsepower for ploughing the land. The horses and pigs fed off barley, and the cows utilised the meadows, so that in general each farm could be a largely self-sufficient entity, exporting corn, wool and mutton but requiring very little in material inputs from the outside world.

It could, however, only function in this way if the farm was sufficiently large for there to be sheep as well as arable, so that the all-important dung transfers could be maintained. In pre-enclosure days the common flocks were shepherded on common pasture land, and each man's portion of the open fields received its share of dung from the folded sheep. The benefits of the system were thus available to everyone, however small his total holding. The grant of an isolated parcel of land in only one part of the parish was no substitute for the loss of these communal rights, with the result that the full sheep-with-corn economy became the preserve of an increasingly restricted number of large farmers employing most of the population as wage labourers. The results of this process of engrossment in Milton Lilbourne have already been noted.

Fyfield Manor Farm, Milton Lilbourne

In order to estimate in a quantitative way the energy inputs and outputs of this system, let us now examine the particular farm in Milton visited by William Cobbett during the harvest of 1826. Cobbett's information must have derived from his friends at Fyfield Manor Farm, where he stayed the night. This was an exceptionally large farm of 460 hectares, mainly arable and pasture, and including a flock of 1,400 sheep (for details, see Table 4.2).

The labour force needed to run such a farm consisted of four kinds of workers:

1   A few unmarried *domestic servants* and others who 'lived-in' with the farmer. They had the benefit of sharing his table and generally the security of at least an annual contract.
2   *Cottagers*, who were permanent employees but received from the farmer only weekly wages and a cottage which was sometimes rent-free.

Table 4.2 Estimates for the land-use pattern, livestock holdings, and work force at Fyfield Manor Farm in 1826.

Land use	Hectares	Work force	Status
Wheat	81	1 farmer	Married, living-in
Barley	125	2 servants	Single women, living-in
Turnips and ley	103	1 groom-gardener	Single man, living-in
Downland pasture	113	2 shepherd's boys	Single, living-in
Water meadow	6	1 head shepherd	Married, cottager
Enclosed meadow	20	3 shepherds	Married, cottagers
Coppice woodland	12	1 head carter	Married, cottager
Total	*460*	7 carters and ploughmen	Married, cottagers
		1 cowman	Married, cottager
Livestock	**Number**	12 labourers	9 married, villagers
		Harvesters and haymakers	Casual, villagers etc.
Sheep	1,400		
Ploughing horses	16	*Total* (excluding casuals)	
Riding horses	2	32 employed persons	
Cows, pigs, poultry	few	98 dependents	
		128 population	

Note: the land use and livestock numbers are based on average yields and stocking rates for the region at this period. The intention is merely to reconstruct in a generalised way typical conditions on a large Wiltshire farm.

Sources: Cobbett 1822, 1826; Davis 1794; Marshall 1798, 1818; Sandell 1975.

3   *Labourers*, whose work was usually not needed in the winter, and who were therefore employed on a weekly or, sometimes, daily basis.
4   *Seasonal casual labour*, including women and children, whose help was indispensable at the two critical periods, hay-making and harvest.

Only at haymaking and harvest—two periods of potential crisis—did the labour force exert a little pressure on the farmer to receive better-than-average wages. At other times the landless population was desperate for work at any price.

The estimates in Table 4.2 show that 32 persons would be employed on the farm throughout the year, which, including their dependents, implies a population of 128 who are directly supported by this farm (about 19% of the parish). The farm itself makes up 32% of the total area of the parish.

The processes that link this population with its resources are shown in Fig. 4.7. The various flows are classified into (a) inputs, principally the energy of human work; (b) outputs, principally food energy; and (c) various other material flows and monetary transactions.

Agricultural inputs: work

Calculation of the annual input of work into Fyfield Manor Farm can, of course, only be attempted through estimates. We know a certain amount about the conditions of work in manufacturing in the early nineteenth century, but rather less about the situation in agriculture, which is

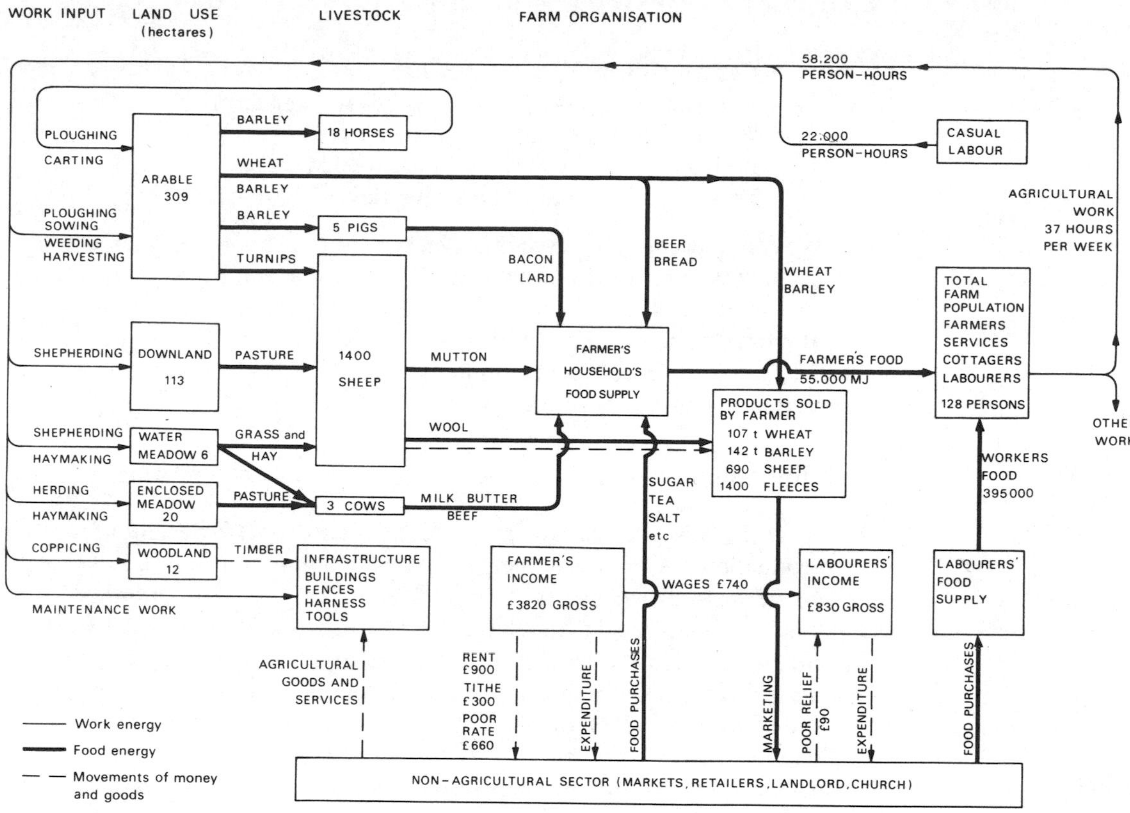

Fig. 4.7 Energy inputs and outputs and material flows in a Wiltshire agricultural system: Fyfield Manor Farm, Milton Lilbourne, 1826.

complicated by great seasonal variations. With arable farming in particular, it was impossible during the winter to work the land during wet or frosty weather, whereas during the summer much less time would be lost in this way. The situation reported by Marshall (1818) for the county of Berkshire seems likely to represent the situation at Milton:

'In the winter, they come to work about seven and stay until about five; and are allowed an hour in the day for meals. In the summer their labour commences at six and ends at six; they are then allowed two hours for meals.'

Boys were employed from the age of ten onwards, but girls and women were usually excluded from farm work except at haymaking and harvest.

When employed, the labourers were therefore expected to put in up to 60 hours or more per week of work, but in the winter they spent many hours unemployed subsisting off Poor Relief. Taking into account the days and hours lost through conditions being unsuitable for work, the workers at Fyfield Manor Farm worked 37.3 hours per week on average, which is about four times the level recorded for the subsistence farmers of New Guinea (Chapter 3).

Using these and other data, the following total labour inputs can be estimated for the productive workers at Fyfield:

12 labourers: 10 hours per day, 5 days per week, 37 weeks per year = 22,200 hours.

18 full-time workers: 8 hours per day, 5 days per week, 50 weeks per year = 36,000 hours.

Casual workers:
Haymaking (26 ha of meadow), 280 worker-days.
Wheat harvest (81 ha), 720 worker-days.
Barley harvest (125 ha), 1,240 worker-days.
Total: 2,240 days at 10 hours per day = 22,400 hours.

We can thus calculate an annual work input of around 80,600 hours of productive farm work, of which 38% was casual employment for haymaking and harvesting (see Fig. 4.7). If we assume, on average, a rate of energy expenditure for agricultural workers of 0.8 MJ per hour, then the total work energy input amounts to 64,480 MJ per year for the farming system as a whole.

Other inputs: horses

As in the New Guinea case, most of the other energy inputs into food production are themselves generated through human effort, and so need not be separately considered. In particular, the enormous amount of human labour saved through the use of horses for ploughing, harrowing and carting, is virtually a 'free' energy input, although made possible by the human work of managing the animals and growing the barley, oats and grass upon which they were fed. Concerning Wiltshire horses, Thomas Davis remarked in 1794: 'as their food, which in general is barley, is taken from the barn unmeasured, the expense of keeping them is seldom exactly known'. For our energy accounting purposes, however, the cost of the barley is clearly the labour cost of producing it.

Replacing his stock of horses would have been one of the major expenses of the Wiltshire farmer, since few horses were bred on farms. Perhaps two colts a year would have been needed, on average. In addition there was a continual need for leather to be used for harness. Few other items needed to be purchased. The farm would have been virtually self-sufficient in fodder for livestock, in timber, and in seed other than for fodder crops like turnip. The ploughs and iron tools would have needed occasional repair, but these items of capital equipment were generally very durable.

The threshing machine

One particular piece of equipment deserves further mention: the threshing machine. Its use was just beginning in the corn country of Southern England, and it became a particular object of hatred among agricultural labourers. The threshing machine represents a further stage in the substitution of animal labour for human labour, and as the threshing of corn was traditionally one of the jobs carried out in the winter irrespective of the weather out of doors, the mechanisation of this task by means of a horse-driven mill was bitterly resented by working people. For the large farmer, however, the savings were considerable. On a farm like Fyfield, the cost of threshing the corn by machine was about one-third the cost of hand threshing, and there was the added advantage of completing the job soon after harvest when corn prices were generally at their highest.

The savings for small farmers were much more marginal, and for them any small advantage was outweighed by the effects of the increased

Harvesting wheat in
industrial Flanders: detail
after Brueghel's
The Harvesters'
(ca 1565).

Using the wage rates of the time, we can calculate that the £100 spent
by the farmer would have provided full-time employment for about 8
artisans and craftsmen, and so would have supported some 40 persons in
total. (This is a similar estimate to that provided by Cobbett (1822), who
wrote that 'the farmer of 400 acres has to pay out of the produce of his
crop ... for about 15 persons including children in the tradesman branch
of the labour performed on his farm, which labour is as necessary to him
as is the labour of the ploughman himself'; using these data it can be
reckoned that Fyfield Manor Farm, with 1,137 acres, would have
supported 43 subsidiary persons.) If the indirect efforts of 8 full-time
artisans and tradesmen are needed to maintain the Fyfield agricultural
system, and if they work on average for 2,500 hours per year each, then
this represents a total work input of 16,000 MJ.

Outputs: food and drink

Some of the food produced at Fyfield was consumed on the farm,
especially the wheat (flour for bread), barley (malt for beer), pigs
(themselves eating barley, for bacon and lard), and dairy products (milk,
butter and cheese). With few exceptions, however, these items were only
eaten in the farmer's household. His workers had to purchase their own
food, apart from a few potatoes and vegetables which they might be able
to grow in their gardens.

Only during the harvest was the farmer expected to provide food for his
workers, in the form of two or three suppers each week. At this time,
however, drink and piece-work were the main incentives provided by the
farmer in order to assemble a large and industrious work force. It is
recorded for the neighbouring county of Dorset that the usual daily
allowance of beer at haytime and harvest was three pints or more for the
women, and seven pints for the men. In Somerset, mowing grass was
rewarded with 1¼ shillings per acre and one gallon of cider; reaping
wheat with 4 shillings per acre and 2½ gallons of cider (Fig. 4.8).

unemployment that resulted from mechanised threshin
number of unemployed people in the parish, the larger
levied on the farmers for the support of these people. N
sympathised with the labourers when, during the 'Cap1
uprising of 1830, the rioters demanded that the use of t
machines be outlawed. In Milton parish in November 1
widespread rioting, rick-burning and robbery, and seve
machines were destroyed. We do not know for certain,
that Fyfield Manor Farm was the focus of some of this

Fossil fuel subsidy

In calculating the energy subsidy required to supply Fy
with these external goods and services, we need to cons
that was involved in their provision. In all cases, huma
have been the major requirement. Even the threshing r
usually the product of full industrial technology. Most
implements and machines were made and repaired by 1
working iron with charcoal and sometimes a little coal

The naturalist W.H. Hudson (1910) provides us with
oral histories about fossil fuel use in early nineteenth-c

'In those days—down to about 1840—it was customar
the cottages, the first cost of which was about four and
wagon load. The cost of its conveyance to the villages
Plain was about five to six shillings a load, as it came f
distance, mostly from the New Forest. . . . A wagon lc
another of faggots lasted him [a shepherd, born about
with the furze obtained from his "liberty" on the dow

The only users of coal were the village blacksmiths. Hu
coal was brought to the villages by itinerant traders usi
sacks being carried by each donkey. A village blacksmi
supplied in this way with the equivalent of about a wag
400 kg) of coal each year. The direct energy cost of thi
11,700 MJ. As Fyfield accounts for 32% of the parish
reasonable to allocate to it the same proportion of tota
would therefore be 3,750 MJ. This energy subsidy amc
2% of the total energy input of the farm, showing that
time was still very much pre-industrial in overall techn

The cost of external labour

For accounting purposes we can disregard the domesti
domestic purchases, but we must take into account the
provide the various goods and services supplied to the
A convenient way to estimate labour is through the mc
these inputs:

Livestock (2 colts)
Leather (80 lb)
Threshing machine (10% depreciation)
Maintenance of implements and ploughs
Miscellaneous items (e.g. turnip seed)

Total external inputs

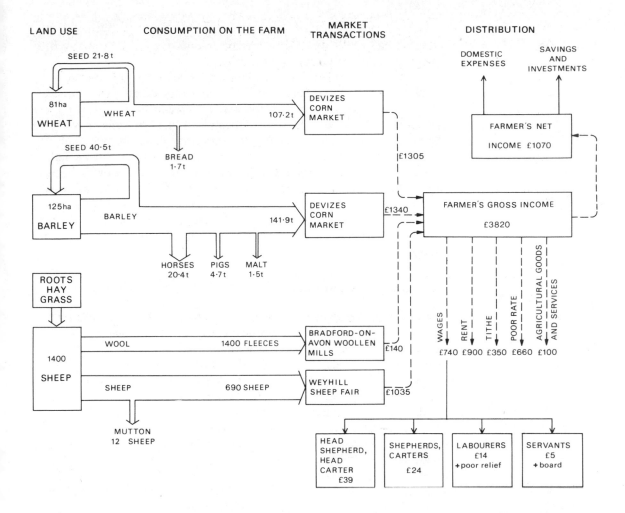

LAND USE	CONSUMPTION ON THE FARM	MARKET TRANSACTIONS	DISTRIBUTION

Fig. 4.9 Economics of farming at Fyfield: main sources of income and expenditure in 1826.

For the rest of the year the workers had to provide food and drink for themselves. Their diet seldom included many of the things that they helped to produce, and most were too poor even to buy woollen clothing. Instead, the bulk of the farm produce was sold. In the angry words of William Cobbett (1826):

'The infernal system causes it all to be carried away. Not a bit of good beef, or mutton, or veal, and scarcely a bit of bacon is left for those who raise all this food and wool ... DEVIZES is the market-town to which the corn goes from the greater part of this valley, ... and the *canal*, that passes close by it, is the great channel through which the produce of the country is carried away to be devoured by the idlers, the thieves, and the prostitutes, who are *all* tax-eaters, in the WENS of Bath and London.'

Rich farmers and poor farmers

The scale of this expropriation can be gauged from Fig. 4.9, which is a reconstruction of the accounts of Fyfield Manor Farm. Wheat, barley and sheep contribute in almost equal proportion to the farmer's gross income of £3,820. Out of this he paid the absentee landlord £900 in rent (about £1 per acre of arable). Another £1,000 was paid to the Church as a tithe, and in the form of Poor Rates. The wage bill amounted to £740, which was distributed amongst the 31 employees according to rank and status. Even so, the farmer's net income amounted to £1,070, almost fifty times the income of most of his employees.

In one respect Fyfield was not typical of farms in the region: it was much larger and so more profitable. Within Milton parish there were 55 owners of land all with holdings less than one-twentieth the size of Fyfield (see Table 4.1). When one considers the impossibility of achieving economies of scale (e.g. manuring, threshing machines) on such small holdings, then it becomes clear that the net incomes of these very small farmers would almost certainly have been less than one-twentieth the net income of Fyfield. The harvest in 1826 was a good one, but in bad years farm incomes might be halved. It is not surprising that many of the smallholders had gone bankrupt in the 1820s, and were forced to become labourers themselves, renting their land to the larger farms or selling it off altogether.

Unemployment and riots

The majority of employers of agricultural labour were therefore in dire financial straits, and could hardly be blamed for paying their workers starvation wages. On the larger farms like Fyfield, which could well afford to increase wages, there was absolutely no economic incentive to do so: labour was plentiful, and if a worker was dissatisfied there were plenty of unemployed men who could replace him.

Admittedly, agricultural wages in Wiltshire, Hampshire and Dorset were the lowest in the country, but everywhere outside the manufacturing regions the situation was almost as bad. Cobbett saw in 1826 that in the Valley of the Avon 'the common people know that they are ill-used, and they cordially, most cordially, hate those who ill treat them'. The situation could not, he felt continue: 'there must be an end to it, and my firm belief is, that that end will be dreadful'.

Cobbett was partly correct in his forecast. Four years later, in 1830, Southern and Eastern England erupted in rioting and destruction. In the Vale of Pewsey and elsewhere in Wiltshire unemployed and under-employed men marched from village to village, burning ricks, breaking threshing machines, and demanding a 10-shilling weekly wage instead of the existing 7½ shillings. However, the uprising was almost wholly non-violent, and it was suppressed without much difficulty by the authorities. For a few years the farmers did pay increased wages, but in Wiltshire the most long-lasting effect of the riots was to postpone for some decades the spread of threshing machines. This postponement did at least do something to preserve the relatively labour-intensive nature of the farming system, but it was hardly the revolution which Cobbett hoped for and many of the ruling class feared.

Efficiency of the system: the energy ratio

Nevertheless, as an aggregate system the efficiency of the farm is impressive when we measure its inputs and outputs in energy terms. The net energy produced by the system in an edible form (wheat, barley, sheep, and subsistence foods such as bacon and dairy products) amounts to 3,398 GJ, 87% in the form of grain. This total output compares to an input of 84.2 GJ, 98% in the form of labour. The energy ratio is therefore

40.3, some three times more favourable than the energy ratio of the Tsembaga Maring of New Guinea, as a result very largely of the use of horses as 'energy slaves'.

We can compute very approximately the work input of the horses, by estimating that on average the arable land will need two ploughings a year, requiring in autumn and winter 50 horse-hours per hectare and in spring and summer 20 horse-hours per hectare. This implies for Fyfield a total input of about 17,000 horse-hours per year, or say 20,000 horse-hours when other tasks are included. Work by horses can be converted into energy by adopting a mean expenditure rate of 8 MJ per hour. If we included this input of horse labour, we would therefore increase the farm's total energy input to 240,000 MJ, so reducing the energy ratio to 14—virtually identical to that of the New Guinea system.

Gross energy productivity

These data suggest that the domestication of animals, and their use as energy slaves in agriculture, is one of the major differences between the two pre-industrial farming systems that we have examined. Compared with the New Guinea example, the Wiltshire farming system has the potential for providing a three times better standard of welfare for its producing population. In reality, as we have seen, the nature of the social organisation that had emerged in England by the early nineteenth century meant that almost all the benefits from the system were expropriated by the tenant farmer, by his landlord, by the Church, and by the urban economy which provided a market for the agricultural products. Cobbett's comments are, as usual, very much to the point:

'Our indignation and rage against this infernal system is not half roused, till we see the *small number of labourers* who raise all the food and drink, and, of course, the mere trifling portion of it that they are suffered to retain for their own use.'

The GEP that we can calculate reinforces this view. On a per capita basis, the gross output of edible crops and animals amounts to 80.3 MJ per day, averaged out over the population of farm workers and their families. This average figure is eight times the average GEP of the Tsembaga Maring of New Guinea, but whereas the egalitarian nature of Maring society gave the mean productivity statistic some relevance, in the Wiltshire case it is a more abstract measure.

Surplus energy income

If we consider the economy of a single farm worker and his family (Fig. 4.10), then the true situation for the majority of the farm population begins to emerge. An average household of one labourer, his wife and three children might earn a total of £30 per year, if we assume some harvest bonus through the casual earnings of the wife and eldest child. The only subsistence income would have come from home-grown vegetables, in particular potatoes, which the labourer cultivated in his spare time on land rented to him by the farmer. At most the garden's produce could only supply 20% of the diet, the remainder of which had to be purchased. Bread was the main item of diet, supplying over half of

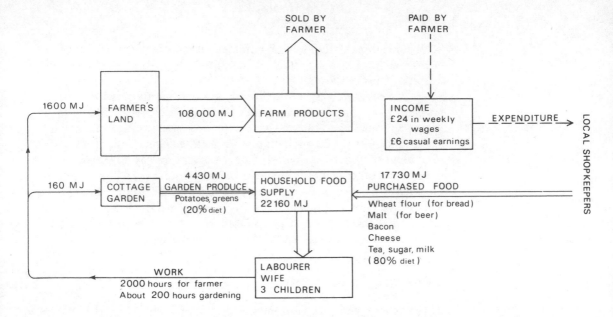

SOLD BY FARMER

PAID BY FARMER

1600 MJ → FARMER'S LAND — 108 000 MJ → FARM PRODUCTS

INCOME
£24 in weekly wages
£6 casual earnings — EXPENDITURE →

LOCAL SHOPKEEPERS

160 MJ → COTTAGE GARDEN

4 430 MJ GARDEN PRODUCE
Potatoes, greens (20% diet)

HOUSEHOLD FOOD SUPPLY 22 160 MJ

17 730 MJ PURCHASED FOOD
Wheat flour (for bread)
Malt (for beer)
Bacon
Cheese
Tea, sugar, milk
(80% diet)

LABOURER WIFE 3 CHILDREN

WORK
2000 hours for farmer
About 200 hours gardening

Fig. 4.10 Energy flows in the cottage economy of a typical Wiltshire labourer of the 1820s.

the food energy. Bacon and a little cheese were the principal supplements, with tea and home-brewed beer to drink. Little or no money would be left for buying such items as cloth (for clothing), leather (for shoes), and oil (for rush lights—most farm workers could not afford candles at this time).

As Fig. 4.10 shows, the average farm worker produced 112,430 MJ per year in food energy, which was five times the amount that he and his family actually consumed—the same disparity that Cobbett had estimated after his visit to Fyfield, using a more approximate method of analysis. If we divide the food energy production of the household by its input of agricultural work energy, we obtain a ratio of 12.6, which is slightly worse than that for the Tsembaga Maring in New Guinea (14.1), and probably a fair reflection of the farm labourer's cottage economy. Whereas the Maring generate an energy surplus which enables them to maintain large pig herds, most Wiltshire labourers were unable to afford enough barley even to support one pig.

However, these calculations misrepresent the position of the labourer's family somewhat, since not quite all their earnings were spent in merely staying alive. Perhaps 20% of their cash income, or £6 per year, would have been retained for non-food purchases. To convert this meagre surplus into a surplus energy income, we need to consider how much food energy could be purchased for every £1 spent. We already know that the other £24 of the household's annual income bought 80% of their total diet, so that the perceived value of the £6 surplus becomes easy to calculate. It amounts to 2.4 MJ per person per day, which is almost identical to the energy value of the surplus crops produced by the Tsembaga Maring (although the two are not strictly comparable since surplus crops can only be used for pig food, whereas surplus money is a more flexible commodity).

Energy yield

When we turn to output per unit area, we find that although it is unproductive by modern standards, the Wiltshire sheep-with-corn economy produces an energy yield which is quite high for the pre-industrial world. The 460 ha of Fyfield Farm generates an average yield of 7,390 MJ per ha in net food energy. The permanent cultivation of the arable land, with the consequent absence of unused fallow, accounts for this system having an energy yield over four times greater than that of the Tsembaga Maring, where the majority of land is under prolonged forest fallow.

Social versus ecological stability

The social instability of English agriculture in the 1820s has already been mentioned. The increasing impoverishment of the labour force due to low wages, and the growing threat posed by low prices to the position of small farmers, resulted in a crisis for rural society, but it was not a crisis which was at all quickly resolved. For most workers the most effective means of improvement in the nineteenth century was always through migration to the industrial towns.

On the other hand, in terms of ecological stability this sheep-and-corn agriculture seems to have been highly successful. Most observers agreed that the main threat to the system lay in a reduced number of sheep and hence less manure for the maintenance of soil fertility. Up until 1870 there was a steady conversion of down land pasture to arable, but it did not result in any great reduction in sheep. The new fodder crops proved to be an adequate replacement for downland pasture, and it was economic and technological changes rather than ecological problems which resulted in the eventual modification of the sheep-and-corn system. Its complete disappearance did not come until a full century after the period that we have been considering.

5 Semi-industrial systems 1 : A Polynesian atoll

South Sea islands: myths and stereotypes

In the early nineteenth century two sets of ideas about the agricultural way of life were current in England. On the one hand many followed Malthus in believing that the rate of reproduction of a well-fed agrarian population was bound to be faster than any possible increase in its means of subsistence. Poverty, vice and misery were the inevitable consequences. Indeed, to improve conditions for agricultural labourers was, in the long term, a self-defeating policy. At the same time, many people felt that at an earlier stage in history, and in exotic parts of the world, rural societies existed which were less subject to inevitable misery. The voyages of Captain Cook in the South Seas did much to stimulate this fantasy of the 'Noble Savage', untainted by civilisation.

In modified form, both sets of beliefs remain part of our intellectual heritage. Perhaps the Noble Savage has receded more than has Malthus, but the South Sea Islands remain a secure refuge for this stereotype. However, for Polynesia there is now enough scientific information for a more balanced view to emerge. It is clear that although the Polynesian setting is more picturesque, the way of life of the agrarian population was not basically any different from any pre-industrial society in the humid tropics, for example New Guinea (Chapter 3).

In this chapter we consider the impact of Western civilisation on Polynesia, through an analysis of how the agricultural system of one small-scale society has responded to industrial technology. The system happens to be located on a group of coral islands (an *atoll*) in the South Pacific. Nevertheless, we shall be dealing with processes of *dependent development* which are the same as those found in any part of the Third World.

We have already seen this phenomenon in an embryo form, with the growing integration of town and countryside in rural Wiltshire 150 years ago (Chapter 4). As William Cobbett (1826) recognised, 'In the Valley of the Avon the people raise nearly twenty times as much food and clothing as they consume, . . . (but) the infernal system causes it all to be carried away.'

The 'infernal system' on Polynesian atolls is represented by the copra trade. Copra (dried coconut) is shipped from many Pacific islands halfway round the world to factories at Port Sunlight on Merseyside, where it is converted into margarine and soap. Some British products still find their way back to the Pacific islands as return trade, for example steel machetes from Birmingham. This reciprocal trade has already persisted for a century, and in this chapter I examine its impact on the agricultural systems which produce the raw materials. When viewed in terms of energy flows, in what ways have these 'semi-industrial' systems of agricultural production been transformed, and who has benefited from the process?

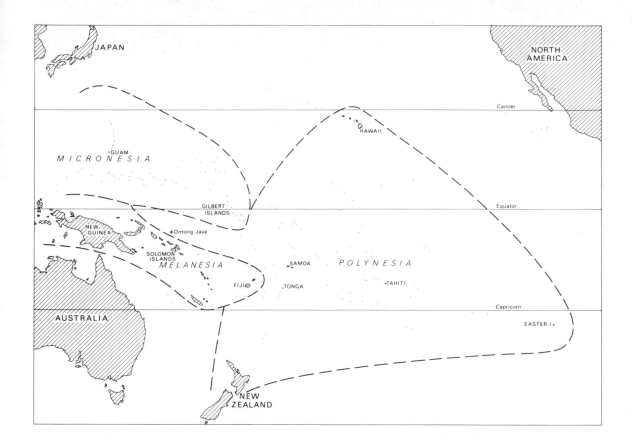

Fig. 5.1 The Polynesian Triangle, showing location of Ontong Java atoll.

Ontong Java atoll, Solomon Islands

The 'Polynesian Triangle' extends from New Zealand in the south to Hawaii in the north Pacific, and as far as Easter Island in the east (Fig. 5.1). Within this region live the speakers of Polynesian dialects, and it formed until five centuries ago the most geographically extensive area with a single language found anywhere in the world. Even to the west of this triangle there are small outliers of Polynesian speakers, probably representing a later phase of settlement by canoe voyagers sailing westwards from the main centres of Polynesian settlement.

Ontong Java atoll to the north of the Solomon Islands represents one such outlier. The atoll itself is large, measuring 70 km from end to end and up to 26 km in width (Fig. 5.2). It consists of 122 different islands, but some are so small that they barely support any vegetation and are overwashed by waves during hurricanes, which, fortunately, are rare events in these latitudes. The islands are constructed by storm waves out of coral limestone debris and sand, and nowhere does the land surface rise more than 4 m above sea level. One is seldom far from the sight and sound of the sea, and in fact all except the largest islands are little more than overgrown beaches (Fig. 5.3).

The total area of vegetated land is a mere 777 hectares, which is almost double the total area of Tsembaga Maring clan territory in New Guinea (Chapter 3), and about half the size of Milton Lilbourne parish in Wiltshire (Chapter 4). In the atoll case, however, as well as the land there are important marine resources, especially in the lagoon. In the sections which follow we shall examine the energy flow and nutrient cycles which

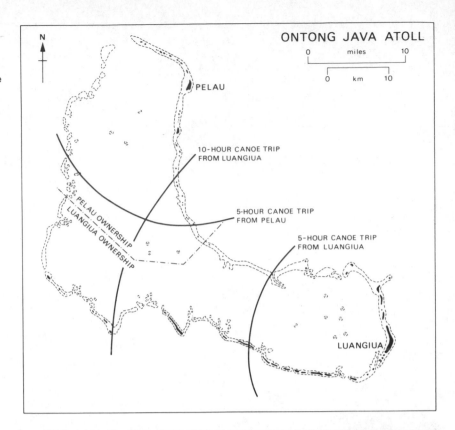

Fig. 5.2 Ontong Java atoll, Solomon Islands, showing average travel times from the two main villages.

ONTONG JAVA ATOLL

PELAU

10-HOUR CANOE TRIP
FROM LUANGIUA

5-HOUR CANOE TRIP
FROM PELAU

5-HOUR CANOE TRIP
FROM LUANGIUA

PELAU OWNERSHIP
LUANGIUA OWNERSHIP

LUANGIUA

Fig. 5.3 The lagoon shore at Luangiua, Ontong Java: a green turtle is being pulled up the beach.

enable the population to achieve a livelihood from this rather restricted and difficult environment.

Atolls: desert islands or oases?

From Captain Cook onwards, European observers of the high volcanic islands of the Pacific had no difficulty in imagining a life of 'primitive affluence' for the inhabitants. On atolls, however, it was a different story:

'They are small low islands level with the water's edge . . . covered with cocoanut trees and dense underwood and inhabited by a poor set of naked wretches who must be sorely straitened for food, as the islands are not much more spacious than a good-sized orchard and the water probably brackish!' (cited by Bayliss-Smith 1977).

This description was written in 1841 by the Ship's Surgeon of a British whaler, and it refers to Takuu, an atoll 240 km to the west of Ontong Java. Similar sentiments are echoed in an academic account by a modern American geographer, W.L. Thomas (1963):

'Coral reefs with their low sandy islets provide the most limited range of resources for human existence and the most tenuous of habitats for man in the Pacific . . . The soil is infertile, lacking humus, and fresh ground water is very limited . . . Maintaining a livelihood is a considerable task for man.'

The picture of atoll life suggested by these writers is one of hardship, but it is worth noting that neither account makes any reference to marine resources. Recent research by biologists suggests what islanders have always known, namely that *coral reefs* are oases of high productivity located in the midst of comparatively barren tropical seas. As such the coral reef provides an interesting parallel to the tropical rain forest: both ecosystems exist in climatically rather stable environments, and have developed over a long period of evolution; both are rich in species, highly productive, but depend upon an efficient and rapid recycling of a limited stock of mineral nutrients for their continued survival. It has been argued that these ecosystems are also rather easy for man to disrupt, but as we saw in New Guinea (Chapter 3) this is not likely to happen with a low intensity of exploitation and with a pre-industrial technology.

Concepts of overpopulation

Ontong Java may have been inhabited since the earliest prehistoric period, over 3,000 years ago. At various times, population pressure was no doubt experienced, but there is some evidence that through practices like induced abortion, abstinence from sexual relations for two years after childbirth, and perhaps in extreme cases infanticide, the population restricted its numbers to below the carrying capacity of the environment. Perhaps nowhere does mankind have such a keen perception of the 'limits to growth' as on small isolated islands, so the existence of conscious measures to ensure resource conservation and population restriction is not altogether surprising.

Before European contact the atoll supported an estimated 2,000 people, but whaling ships and traders in the nineteenth century introduced diseases, notably influenza and malaria, which had catastrophic effects. The population declined up until 1940, when only 580 people remained. Since then there has been a recovery. In 1970 when I visited Ontong Java to do research the population numbered 860, and there were a further 200 migrants who had been born on the atoll but had migrated to the main Solomon Islands.

In terms of basic food supply overpopulation has not been a real threat on Ontong Java for over a century, but the society is now subject to new kinds of scarcity, as the atoll economy has become more and more dependent on trade. The monetary economy induces scarcity, by stimulating a demand for new imported goods: rice, sugar, tea, tobacco, soap, alcohol.

Since the 1950s there have been new employment opportunities in the Solomon Islands, and instead of working for money at home increasing numbers of young people now leave the atoll in order to seek their fortunes elsewhere, working for wages in the towns and on the plantations. The scale of this out-migration reflects the fact that some people see no way of satisfying their new aspirations without leaving home for at least a period of their lives. It is the quality of life which an area can give, rather than its capacity to provide subsistence, which gives us the most reliable measure of 'overpopulation'. In this sense Ontong Java is again becoming overpopulated.

The original egalitarian society?

In the traditional economy the most important products were foodstuffs, in particular fish and taro. These items were valuable because of the labour and skill needed to produce them, but they were not capable of being hoarded in the way that money is. The best way to use any surplus products is to give them away, and so enhance one's status. Such generosity is not entirely disinterested: there is always some expectation that, at a future date, the gift will be reciprocated, but at the same time it is recognised that some individuals are in a better position to give away certain things than are others. For example, a skilled fisherman will gain status by distributing to his kinsfolk fish, and in return his household might receive woven mats, baskets, or other foods like taro. This network of reciprocal exchange is one way in which a society of equals tends to emerge in most small-scale communities. Even the possibility of accumulating visible wealth in the form of pig herds, as in New Guinea, was denied to atoll dwellers, whose only domestic animals were dogs and rats!

The sheer impossibility on atolls of generating any great surplus of anything of value is another reason for the rather equal distribution of wealth and status. On the high islands of Polynesia, with relatively plentiful land resources, quite elaborate stratified societies emerged, such as the aristocracy of priests and chiefs with whom Captain Cook had dealings on Tahiti. On atolls, however, the resource base did not permit such elaborate social distinctions. Moreover, atoll resources are subject to catastrophic reduction as a result of droughts and hurricanes. The anthropologist Marshall Sahlins has argued that the social organisation of atolls such as Ontong Java is an adaptation to these problems of endemic shortage and occasional famine. Instead of the household being the sole unit of social affiliation, there is a variety of alternative groups with which the individual can associate, for fishing, house-building, copra-making and so forth. Whatever its origins, this system has the effect of efficiently distributing people among the available resources, thus reducing to a minimum social and economic distinctions.

Despite almost a century of copra trading and the use of money on an increasing scale, this broadly egalitarian society still persists on Ontong Java. Money is generally used only for the buying and selling of imported goods, and then only between persons who are not related. Most transactions involving food still take place under the system of reciprocal exchange whereby the individual achieves status through his generosity in distributing goods, rather than through his astuteness in accumulating them.

Will the social organisation of Ontong Java be transformed in the future into the capitalist system that in Chapter 4 we saw exemplified in nineteenth-century England? There land and labour were mere commodities, bought and sold in a free market, and the possession (or inheritance) of capital was the main route towards the achievement of individual wealth and status. Production for the market certainly permits a rapid transformation of a society towards one dominated by capitalist ethics, but the process is not inevitable. In places like Ontong Java a century of involvement with the market economy has not yet resulted in the emergence of acute social stratification, but perhaps the first steps along this road have already been taken.

Food production

Traditionally food on atolls meant one of three things: taro, fish or coconut. The coconut palm thrives under atoll conditions, but all other crops are grown with difficulty. Atoll soils are highly alkaline and have a very low humus content, consisting mainly of carbonate sand and coral debris. An adequate soil for taro can only be achieved by the deliberate accumulation of vegetable compost, preferably under semi-anaerobic conditions of waterlogging so that the rate of breakdown of organic matter is greatly reduced. Both species of taro that are grown on atolls are planted in artificial swamps, usually shallow depressions excavated down to groundwater level and filled with soil derived from vegetable mulch.

Only the larger islands are sufficiently wide for fresh water to accumulate, even on atolls with a high rainfall like Ontong Java. The smaller islands have saline groundwater, and so cannot support taro cultivation. Land for taro is therefore restricted: on Ontong Java only 5% of the land area is suitable, and most of this land is still intensively cultivated, mainly by women. Production of taro provided 29% of food energy in the diet in 1970, compared to 21% from coconut (Fig. 5.4).

Apart from taro and coconut there are few other vegetable crops, but on nutrient-enriched soils close to houses a few sweet potatoes, bananas and sugar cane are also grown. The total contribution of these crops is only about 3% of the diet, but any source of variety is welcome.

Marine resources provide most of the protein in the diet and 19% of the energy, mostly in the form of fish. Many marine invertebrates such as shellfish and octopus are eaten, but quantitatively they are not important. The shell of one mollusc, trochus, provides the only supplementary source of cash income. The mother-of-pearl found inside these gastropod shells finds a market in Hong Kong for the making of buttons and costume jewellery.

The remainder of the Ontong Java diet derives from imports, but even here the variety of foods is not considerable. Money is never sufficient to allow much expenditure on tinned meat or fresh vegetables such as onions, and most of the 25% of the diet that derives from purchased food is from rice, sugar, flour, and navy biscuits. In many ways these carbohydrates act as substitutes for taro in the diet: by collecting coconuts

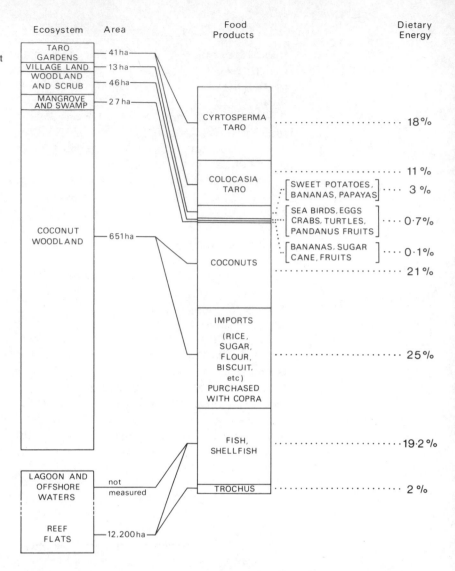

Fig. 5.4 Areas under different land uses, and their contribution to the Ontong Java diet.

and selling them as copra, the people are able to purchase dietary substitutes for their own root crops and thus save themselves the trouble of growing them. As we shall see, this exchange is far from being an equal one from an energy point of view.

Work inputs

Surveys of the daily activities of a random sample of islanders enables us to estimate the total work inputs of men and women into different sectors of the economy (Fig. 5.5). How much productive work is done by each individual varies somewhat, particularly between men and women, but the average for all adults is estimated at 27 hours per week for men and 20 hours for women. Old people and women with young children work less than the average, and individuals in households with many dependents will do rather more, but overall it is clear that Ontong Java lies intermediate in labour intensity between New Guinea subsistence (Chapter 3) and early nineteenth-century Wiltshire (Chapter 4).

As in New Guinea, there is no seasonal peak in labour demands at the time of harvest, since almost all of the food resources are exploited on a

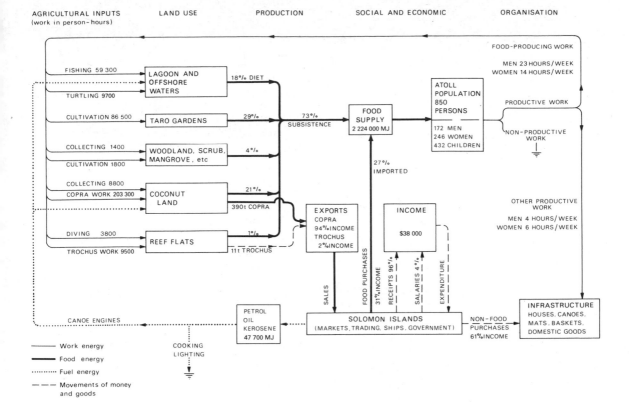

Fig. 5.5 Energy inputs and outputs and material flows in the Ontong Java agricultural system.

continuous basis. Food-producing work makes up the bulk of the total work-load. For men, collecting coconuts, processing them for copra, and fishing are the main occupations; for women, copra work and taro cultivation are the main tasks. For both men and women some time is also taken up in canoe travel between islands. In terms of its energy equivalent, the total work input amounts to 361 GJ per year.

External energy subsidies

The outside world subsidises the Ontong Java economy in two important ways:

1 The market economy provides goods which are imported by the islanders in exchange for their copra income. In the economic sphere the most important of these inputs is petrol, used for powering the outboard motors used by some fishermen on their canoes. The 200 gallons that were used in 1970–1 represent 32 GJ in energy subsidy.

2 There is also an energy cost incurred in providing the shipping links whereby trade is maintained. In the year 1970–1 10 vessels were sent by trading companies in the Solomon Islands to fetch copra and sell goods to the islanders. Data from elsewhere suggest an average energy cost, for coastal shipping, of 0.2 MJ to carry 1 tonne of cargo a distance of 1 km, to which we must add some labour costs. For the 289 tonnes of copra shipped out of Ontong Java in 1970–1, we can calculate an approximate total energy cost of 445 GJ.

The total energy input can therefore be computed as follows:

Work	361 GJ
Fuel subsidy	32 GJ
Transport of copra	445 GJ

Work thus represents only 43% of the total energy input, a clear indication that Ontong Java is now firmly in the 'semi-industrial' category of agricultural systems.

Coconut dependence

The links between Ontong Java and the industrial world operate largely through the copra trade. The making and selling of copra occupies over half of all productive work, and the coconut palm completely dominates the landscape of the atoll: 84% of the land area is planted with coconuts, although not all the nuts are used, especially not from the more remote islands. Many coconuts are eaten, but the bulk are sold as copra, a product rich in vegetable oil and therefore with a high energy value. At one time Pacific Islanders did their own processing and sold crude coconut oil to the traders, but since the 1880s the processing has been done by factories in the industrialised countries. Unilever is the company which purchases most of the copra from the Solomon Islands, where they also manage a few of their own coconut plantations.

On Ontong Java 94% of the total cash income came from selling copra. About one-third of this money was spent on imported foods, which make up 25% of the total diet. The remainder was mostly spent on consumer items (e.g. cigarettes, clothing, towels, soap), and on household goods such as pots and pans, knives, tools and paint. Kerosene and petrol were still cheap in 1970, and constituted only 1% of total expenditure. On the other hand, this limited use of fossil fuels does represent the first tentative steps towards the more complete dependence which, as we shall see later, characterises fully industrialised systems of food production.

Energy yields from land and sea

Four types of ecosystem are exploited on the atoll: taro gardens, coconut land, woodland, and coral reefs (see Fig. 5.4).

The areas exploited and their outputs of food energy are shown in Table 5.1. It is clear from these energy yield data that the idea of atolls as desert islands is completely false. Even if we include in the total land area the virtually unexploited areas such as mangrove forest and beach scrub, even so the total food energy yield from the land amounts to 14,760 MJ per hectare, at least eight times the level of yield achieved from tropical rain forests by the Tsembaga Maring (Chapter 3), and double the net energy yield from the ecologically efficient sheep-and-corn husbandry of Wiltshire (Chapter 4). At 16,000 MJ/ha, the intensively cultivated taro swamps on the atoll have a similar yield to the land under coconuts, despite the latter being extensively managed or even totally neglected. However, whereas the taro is all eaten by the atoll population, the energy from coconuts is mostly destined for consumption by the industrialised countries.

The yield from marine ecosystems is less easy to assess than that of the terrestrial resources. As we have seen, most of the output from the sea is

Table 5.1 Energy yields of different ecosystems of Ontong Java atoll.

Category of land use	Area (hectares)	Food energy output (MJ)	Yield (MJ/ha)
Taro gardens	40.7	652,080	16,022
Coconut land	651.1	10,749,900	16,510
Other land (village plots, scrub, swamp, woodland, mangrove)	85.8	80,010	933
Total land area	778	11,481, 990	14,758
Coral reefs and reef flats	12,224	428,840	35

in the form of fish. Since most fish are found in the vicinity of coral reefs, and since we can estimate the area of reefs from air photographs, an approximate yield figure can be calculated. Not surprisingly this average yield, 35 MJ/ha, is comparatively low. Not only are some areas of the lagoon rather inaccessible to fishermen, and so some reefs are almost unexploited, but also we are comparing a hunting/gathering economy (fishing and collecting shellfish) with an agricultural technology on land. Animal protein is always an 'expensive' food in energy terms, and a fairer comparison would be with pig husbandry in New Guinea (Chapter 3). The Tsembaga Maring gained 3.2 energy units in pork for every one unit of associated work, whereas Ontong Java fishermen gain 8.6 units in fish per unit expended in fishing. Once again, the atoll environment is shown to be much more favourable than its reputation would suggest.

Sailing canoes as energy slaves

This impressive yield of food energy from the atoll ecosystem is achieved without the direct assistance of 'energy slaves' such as the horses whose contribution in nineteenth-century English farming we have already examined (Chapter 4). The only significant natural energy subsidy is wind power harnessed by the sailing canoes, which has the effect of greatly reducing the 'friction of distance' by permitting rapid transport of personnel and goods from one part of the atoll to another (Fig. 5.6).

Efficient transport is made necessary by the very scattered nature of the atoll's resources and because the population occupies only two permanent settlements which are at opposite ends of the atoll (see Fig. 5.2). Temporary settlements therefore have to be established on the more remote islands, so that fish or coconuts or timber can be obtained without too much loss of time through travelling. Adults spend about ten weeks a year, on average, living away from the main villages.

As a result of these adaptations, the actual 'friction of distance' is surprisingly small. The time needed to construct and maintain canoes (3% of total work), and the time involved in travelling between islands (6.5% of total work), when averaged out over the adult population amounts to only 1.7 hours per person per week. This is a very modest investment of time by comparison with the 'journey to work' in other societies.

Fig. 5.6 Sailing canoes leave Luangiua village for a day's fishing in the lagoon.

If outboard engines were to be adopted instead of sails, then the islanders could 'commute' to the outlying islands on a daily basis whatever the weather. In this way they could enjoy the social benefits of living permanently in the two central villages, but at the same time obtain access without effort to the resources of the more remote islands. In the long run such a change is, perhaps, inevitable, but until the capital investment has been made and the necessary mechanical skills have been acquired, then the 'intermediate technology' of sailing canoes is likely to remain dominant.

The energy ratio

The energy ratio is found by dividing the energy outputs (subsistence food + copra exports) by all the energy inputs that derive from human activities (work + engine fuel + transport costs). The dependence on trade of the Ontong Java system means that the exported energy (10,292 GJ) greatly exceeds the subsistence food consumption (1,619 GJ), but the input is also greatly boosted by fossil fuel consumption. The overall ratio is therefore 14.2 units of output per unit of input, which is no better than the efficiency of the New Guinea system (Chapter 3) despite the large export of energy that Ontong Java achieves.

Gross energy productivity

The difference between these two systems is revealed by the GEP, which for Ontong Java amounts to 38.4 MJ, four times that of the self-sufficient New Guinea cultivators, but only two-thirds the level achieved by the Wiltshire farm of 1826 (Chapter 4).

If in 1970 the resources of Ontong Java had been more fully exploited, then the GEP would be somewhat larger. Copra production in the early 1960s averaged 480 tonnes per year, compared with only 389 tonnes in 1970–1. In 1967 a hurricane devastated the coconut palms on about half the islands of the atoll, and by 1970 yields had still not recovered fully. In a more favourable year there would probably be little difference between

Ontong Java and Wiltshire in GEP. Both are probably close to the limits that their respective environments can produce under a largely pre-industrial technology.

Surplus energy income

One interesting difference between these two systems is revealed by the measure of surplus energy income. In both cases the bulk of food energy produced is exported to distant markets, so that a measure of income is required which corresponds more closely to the actual standard of living of the people than does the energy productivity statistic. As in Wiltshire, the Ontong Java population has a surplus cash income in addition to the money used for subsistence, and we can calculate the amount of food energy that this surplus money would buy if we know the actual pattern of expenditure on imported food and its financial cost. In 1970–1 the surplus income per caput amounted to 33 Australian dollars, which was the equivalent of 5.3 MJ per person per day in food energy.

This surplus energy income on Ontong Java is over twice the level computed for the Wiltshire farm worker's household, although if an average figure for Wiltshire could be calculated—which included the farmer as well as his labourers—then much of the difference would no doubt disappear. More significantly, it is over twice the level computed for the Tsembaga Maring (Chapter 3). We can envisage Ontong Java society as having progressed over the last century from an economy of complete self-sufficiency, like that of the Maring, to their current mixed economy where a substantial subsistence component is combined with the production of a cash crop exported in exchange for imported food and other goods. Up until 1970 this transition to a 'semi-industrial' agricultural economy seems to have led to an improvement in welfare, as the surplus energy income figure suggests, but since that time the problems of economic dependence have emerged in much starker form.

Hurricanes: a natural hazard

For some families on the atoll, the problems inherent in a dependent agricultural economy first became apparent in 1967, in the wake of Cyclone Annie. This hurricane completely destroyed the coconuts on certain islands, so that for some families the major source of their cash income was completely eliminated. The traditional rules of social organisation would have enabled persons in these families to obtain access to coconuts growing on other islands that were not so badly damaged, by affiliating themselves with distant relations who had land rights there. Today, however, the rights of affiliation are much less flexible. The new ideology stresses the exclusive ownership by families of resources like coconuts which belong primarily to the monetary sector.

For the first time, therefore, the period after the hurricane saw a polarisation between the rich and poor households. Since most of the diet derives from subsistence foods which were still plentiful, there was no danger of actual starvation in those families whose copra resources had been destroyed. In any case the traditional network of reciprocal exchange would not allow such a thing to happen. But to receive gifts without being able to reciprocate them places the individual in an embarrassing position. Rather than accept charity from families whose cash income was relatively unaffected by the hurricane, many of the needy families emigrated to find wage employment in the Solomon Islands. Others tightened their belts and retreated to a subsistence livelihood, awaiting the time when their coconut palms would recover and enable them to participate once more in the market economy.

Postscript, 1986

In the 1970s that market economy itself entered into a period of crisis as a result of the realisation by Middle East oil producers that they were selling a scarce and diminishing resource to industrialised countries increasingly dependent on it. One result of oil price rises was a massive inflation in the price of manufactured goods and food, but these price increases were not matched by any significant rise in the price of most primary commodities, especially those derived from the agricultural sector of the Third World. The producers of commodities like copra are in no position to dictate the terms of trade, which became steadily more unfavourable during the 1970s. What has been the response of the islanders to this threat?

A return visit to Ontong Java in 1986 enabled me to collect some up-to-date information which showed that the atoll economy has been remarkably resilient. The lagoon has proved to be a rich source of sea slugs or *beche-de-mer*, which in dried form are now exported from the Solomon Islands to places like Hong Kong and Singapore where they are in demand as a gourmet food. For some years now *beche-de-mer* has been more important than copra as a source of income on Ontong Java. This new wealth has encouraged a further shift towards imported foods. In 1986 51% of the diet derived from imports compared to 25% in 1970–71, even though the population has now grown to 1,400 people.

The large sums earned from *beche-de-mer* have also financed a large investment in fibre-glass canoes and outboard engines, thus tightening still further the dependence of the people on the technology of the outside world. In 1970–71 each person used on average only 1.1 litres of petrol per year, but by 1986 per capita consumption had grown to 122.4 litres. Over one hundred engines were in use, almost entirely replacing the sailing canoes that were the pride and joy of the previous generation of fishermen. If we assume, as an approximation, that engine depreciation and maintenance entails energy costs equivalent to 40% of fuel energy expenditure, then an Energy Ratio of 1.04 can be calculated for 1986. The growth in outputs from the atoll (exports, subsistence foods) in no way matches the vast increase in energy input, of which only 5% is now in the form of human labour. Ontong Java has now entered the full-industrial age in its energy use patterns, despite preserving a social structure largely inherited from the pre-industrial past.

6 Semi-industrial systems 2 : The Green Revolution in South India

Green Revolution: filling the half-empty rice bowl?

In the world as a whole, three out of five people depend upon rice as their staple food. Most of these rice-eaters live in Monsoon Asia, the crescent of countries that extends from Pakistan through India and South-east Asia to China and Japan. In this chapter we shall examine rice cultivation in South India, focusing in particular on the complex of technological changes that has occurred since the late 1960s, and which has been termed the Green Revolution.

Its proponents claimed that the Green Revolution was going to lead to spectacular increases in crop yields as a result of the adoption by farmers of new crop varieties such as 'miracle rice', IR 8, together with a more modern technology. As a result the living standards of rural people were to be substantially improved, as more food and more money became available. For a few years many people believed, in the words of one expert, that 'the development of IR 8 and its dissemination throughout Asia is literally helping to fill hundreds of millions of rice bowls once only half full'. This optimistic attitude was summed up as follows by the Indian economist, K. Mukerji (1974):

'If there has not been a Green Revolution just yet [in 1972], the technology of Green Revolution is knocking at the door. It is a technology that involves hybrid seeds, high fertiliser dosages, use of pesticides, and so on. All that is necessary is to open the door. That is all.'

Opening this door has, however, proved to be not at all straightforward, and unfortunately in South India the result of doing so has not been the filling up of millions of half-empty rice bowls. A few are now overflowing, it is true, but many are no fuller than before and some are becoming emptier. In 1972 Mukerji recognised that in India 'the geographical location of the Green Revolution patches as well as its patchiness has always been somewhat suspicious'. Five years later the geographer B.H. Farmer (1977) was describing the original Green Revolution ideology as 'a cruel and facile optimism':

'We have descended once again into gloom and despondency . . . There is a large question-mark . . . against the Green Revolution as a means of overcoming in the longer term the basic South Asian problems of food supply and increasingly intolerable poverty. The question-mark hangs heavily over the Green Revolution in general, over wheat and the millets as well as rice. But it hangs heaviest of all over rice.'

In this chapter we shall be considering the reality behind these rather sweeping statements. To what extent has paddy rice agriculture in South India been converted successfully into a more modern (and hence more industrialised) system of food production? And who has benefited from this process? We shall answer these questions by examining the functioning of village-scale agricultural systems both before and after the Green Revolution. Initially, though, we must consider the ecological basis of these agricultural systems which are now being transformed.

The wet paddy ecosystem

In his classic account of the agricultural systems of Java, Clifford Geertz (1963) commented

'The micro-ecology of the flooded paddy field has yet to be written ... The most striking feature of the ecosystem and the one most in need of explanation, is its extraordinary stability or durability, the degree to which it can continue to produce, year after year, and often twice in one year, a virtually undiminished yield ... The answer to this puzzle almost certainly lies in the paramount role played by water in the dynamics of the rice terrace.'

Subsequent research has supported this conclusion, by showing that flowing water is indeed the primary means whereby nutrients are supplied to the ecosystem and maintained within it. Whereas the shifting cultivator manipulates the rain-forest ecosystem, the paddy rice farmer tranforms a dry-land system into an aquatic one. This transformed ecosystem can supply him with a more secure long-term yield (Fig. 6.1).

In various ways the agricultural system itself supplies nutrients, for example through the silt which is transported by the irrigation water, much of which is run-off from surrounding catchments. Even if this silt is deposited mainly in the irrigation ditches, when these are cleaned it will find its way onto the fields. The water also contains dissolved nutrients, the product of chemical weathering in the catchment and of the breakdown of organic detritus. These nutrient inputs are of course supplemented by the farmer, who in South Asia typically adds 10–15 cart-loads per hectare of farmyard manure, as well as ashes, straw, alluvium, and sometimes green compost from leguminous crops. All these supplements are ploughed into the soil before the field is flooded.

Soil changes after flooding

As well as these external inputs, processes occurring within the paddy ecosystem lead to an enhanced supply of nutrients. Waterlogging leads to three kinds of change in the soil: physical, biological and chemical. The physical changes result from the saturation of the pore spaces in the soil, which leads to a swelling of mineral particles and a breakdown in the normal soil structure. This process is accentuated when the farmer and his animals work the soil under waterlogged conditions, which causes 'puddling'. When this happens the soil becomes less and less pervious, so that the leaching of nutrients by downward percolating water is minimised. A second result is that the structural aggregates in the soil are completely destroyed, and it becomes a sort of sludge with the consistency of pea soup. In this puddled soil the exchange of air between atmosphere and soil is minimised, so creating an anaerobic (oxygen-deficient) environment for roots, the so-called *reduced zone*. Only the top 1–10 mm of soil absorbs oxygen from the water, and so forms an *oxidised zone* where processes are comparable to normal dry-land soils (Fig. 6.2).

Fig. 6.1 A peasant farmer lifting water from a well in order to maintain the water level in his rice paddy (North Arcot District, South India).

Fig. 6.2 Outline of the nitrogen cycle in a flooded paddy terrace.

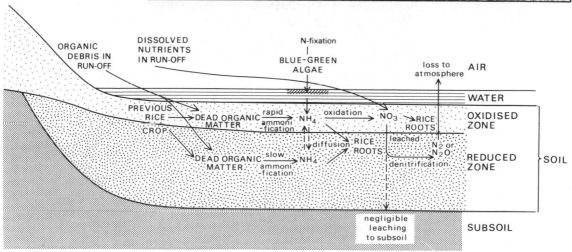

Anaerobic conditions lead to important biological changes. In the absence of oxygen there are drastic changes in the kind of micro-organisms that can survive. These micro-organisms decompose organic matter in the soil and release plant nutrients, a process which occurs particularly rapidly in an oxidised soil under tropical conditions of warmth and humidity. After waterlogging, however, the rate of decomposition declines very sharply. Moreover, there are important changes in the nitrogen cycle (see Fig. 6.2).

In the absence of flooding, and also within the oxidised zone of a flooded field, the normal nitrogen cycle is as follows. The nitrogen in organic matter (dead roots and shoots, manure, soil humus, etc.) is changed during decomposition to an ammonium form (NH_4+), which is unstable and is quite rapidly oxidised to nitrate (NO_3-). Nitrate is not held by soil particles, and unless absorbed by plant roots it is quickly leached or denitrified into a gaseous form, and so is lost to the atmosphere. Because of the abundant micro-organisms present in oxidised soils in the tropics, oxidation and subsequent denitrification occur very rapidly, and nitrogen deficiency soon becomes critical. As a result farmers must shift their cultivation to new land, or alternatively they must replenish continually the supply of organic matter.

Paddy farmers manage to avoid this drain on their nitrogen reserves. With waterlogging the decomposition rate of organic matter slows down, and the rate at which ammonia oxidises into unstable nitrate is minimised. Most of the nitrogen taken up by the rice crop comes from the gradual ammonification of soil organic matter, but there are also some additional sources. One of the most important is the atmospheric nitrogen fixed by blue-green algae (see Fig. 6.2).

The flooded rice field forms an ideal habitat for these microscopic plants. Initially, when the crop is first planted, green algae colonise the water, but after the rice plants have grown sufficiently to provide some shade, the green algae are replaced by blue-green types which form slime colonies, films and such like. Blue-green algae remain dominant so long as water remains in the field, despite almost complete shading by rice plants in the later stages of growth. According to some estimates, as much as 16 tonnes per hectare fresh weight of algae may accumulate, containing as much as 100 kg of nitrogen. This amount greatly exceeds the normal doses of chemical fertiliser that peasant farmers scatter on their fields. Scientists at the International Rice Research Institute in the Philippines have found that artificial fertiliser actually inhibits the activity of the blue-green algae. What is more, other N-fixing organisms also exist, particularly in the root zone of the rice crop. In the absence of rice plants these other micro-organisms are much less frequently present.

Purely chemical changes also follow from waterlogging. From the farmer's point of view the most important is an increased availability of phosphorus, which after nitrogen is the most important plant nutrient. Flooding results in iron, aluminium, manganese and calcium becoming more soluble, and as a result these elements chemically release the phosphorus which under aerated, dry-soil conditions is chemically bound up with them. In normally acid soils (typical in South India) flooding will also reduce acidity. With a higher soil pH the element phosphorus (and others) becomes more available for absorption by plant roots.

Irrigation is therefore a key factor in increasing food energy yields in the tropics, since it leads to the enhanced availability of nutrients and their perpetual replenishment, for as long as an intermittent supply of water can be assured. But unfortunately only two major crops are adapted to fully waterlogged conditions. One is taro *(Colocasia esculenta)*, the root crop which enables dense populations to subsist on many Pacific islands (Chapter 5). The second and more important is rice, the principal basis for the numerous agrarian civilisations of South and East Asia. With shifting cultivation on dry soils, population growth results in a deterioration of the habitat, but under a wet-rice regime population growth leads to the technical elaboration of the same agricultural system within an undamaged habitat. The attempt to transplant industrial technology into this milieu through the Green Revolution must be viewed against the background of the regime's fundamental ecological stability, made possible by agricultural expertise gained during millenia of pre-industrial management.

South India: the need for irrigation

To understand the changing agricultural ecology of South India, I shall examine the functioning at two points in time of a single small-scale system. In both cases the energy inputs are semi-industrial in character, but one case study pre-dates the Green Revolution, whereas the other illustrates its effects. The village chosen is Wangala in Mandya District of Karnataka (formerly Mysore) State, which was studied by the economist/anthropologist Scarlett Epstein in 1955.

Mandya is situated towards the southern margin of the Deccan Plateau of South India, about 100 km from the city of Mysore. The plateau consists of ancient crystalline rocks which are quite deeply weathered, and in the areas that concern us form quite gentle relief. The soils are mainly red loams and clays, thin on the ridges but deep in the valleys as a result of slope-wash under the intense rainfall characteristic of the monsoon.

The climate of this region is dominated by the monsoon. There are four arid months at the beginning of the year followed by the three marginally wet months of the ineffective south-west monsoon. The only truly wet months are those of the retreating monsoon, in the period August–November. The main rice crop is transplanted in July, just before the onset of the reliable monsoon rains, and is harvested in December after the dry season has started.

In this climate, where temperatures are always favourable for plant growth, solar radiation is at a maximum in the dry season and at a minimum during the overcast weather of the monsoon. On the other hand rainfall is generally insufficient to support continuous plant growth except in the four wettest months. Originally, then, this inland region of South India had a savanna-type vegetation and a mixed economy based on pastoralism and an annual crop of finger millet or sorghum. Paddy rice cultivation was restricted to flooded valley bottoms and a few patches of land capable of being irrigated from 'tanks', reservoirs formed by damming ephemeral streams (Fig. 6.3). Not until irrigation was available on a larger scale could farmers extend the growing season from four months to eight or even 12 months. In the southern part of Karnataka (Mysore) State irrigation works were begun by the British administration early this century: Wangala along with 1,600 other villages received water

Fig. 6.3 A village tank in North Arcot, South India, midway through the dry season: bullocks are grazing around the edge of the reservoir.

from canals that were completed in the 1930s, and immediately farmers were presented with new opportunities to grow irrigated crops, particularly rice and sugar cane. Elsewhere in South India local tanks remained the most important source of irrigation water until the introduction of electric pump sets in the 1950s. These machines enabled the area of 'wet' land once again to be extended.

Without irrigation, therefore, rice would be a difficult crop to grow in South India except in a few naturally wet sites. Irrigation was thus the forerunner of the Green Revolution in this region, but as we shall see it is not a sufficient pre-condition for the successful modernisation of rice farming.

Wangala village in 1955

The village studied by Scarlett Epstein (1962) is on the undulating plateau country known as the Maidan. It is a striking landscape at any season of the year:

'In the summer months long stretches of bare red soil show paddy and ragi [millet] fields under the plough; some summer crops and sugar cane of varying height are interspersed between acres of waste and ploughed soil. During the monsoon season the bright green paddy and ragi crops seen against the background of the red soil and inter-mingled with the blue blossoms of the sugar cane present a colourful picture. In the winter the yellowing crops herald the harvest season.'

In Wangala, as well as the arable land under perennial cultivation (243 hectares), there are also 219 hectares of waste land, mostly hill-tops and ridges with soils too eroded to support agriculture, but used by the villagers as rough grazing (Fig. 6.4). The village itself (population 958) is typical of other 'wet' villages in the area. Its economy centres around agriculture, but whereas before the 1930s only 12% of arable land was irrigated, and that unreliably from a local tank liable to run dry, in more recent decades the land-use pattern has been transformed. In 1939 the village was linked by canal to the Krishnaraja Reservoir, and the roads

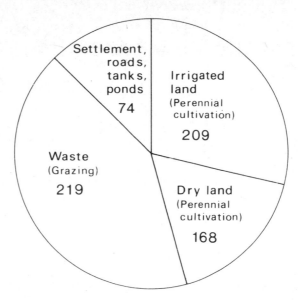

Fig. 6.4 Land use at Wangala in 1955 (in hectares).

Settlement, roads, tanks, ponds 74

Irrigated land (Perennial cultivation) 209

Waste (Grazing) 219

Dry land (Perennial cultivation) 168

leading to local market towns were also improved. The result was an 'agricultural revolution' as profound if not more so than the more recent Green Revolution. It involved the transition from a pre-industrial agrarian society dependent on dry-land crops grown for subsistence, to a society where farmers have become increasingly innovative in technology and capitalist in mode of production, with wet-land crops (sugar cane and rice) as their main source of livelihood.

A stagnant social structure

Despite these changes in agriculture, the social organisation of Wangala remained highly 'traditional' during this period. Indeed, the caste structure of the village was one factor which made possible the development of capitalist farming. Agricultural entrepreneurs need capital, land and labour, especially the last two, in the early phases of the adoption of semi-industrial technology. Two-thirds of the population of Wangala village belong to the Peasant Caste, owning almost nine-tenths of the land. The current rich farmers in Wangala are Peasant men who had enterprise, enough land, and a little working capital, and who, in 1939, discovered suddenly an opportunity to make large profits out of the new cash crops, sugar cane and rice. To be able to exploit these crops the farmer needed to have irrigated land, cheap labour, access to bullock power and, in the case of cane, an investment in fertiliser.

The means to benefit from irrigation was therefore not open to all members of the community. In particular, households with insufficient irrigated land or with no land at all had little option but to work for the large farmers, many of whom were able to reinvest their profits by buying more land from poorer people who had fallen into debt. As the rich got richer, many of the poor became poorer, especially the members of low castes or 'outcastes' like the Untouchables who had never had much land in the first place. The process of differentiation was made worse by steady population growth and by the small number of alternative jobs available in the vicinity.

As in eighteenth-century Britain (Chapter 4), the 'technological' changes were slight (in Wangala, irrigation, access to markets and

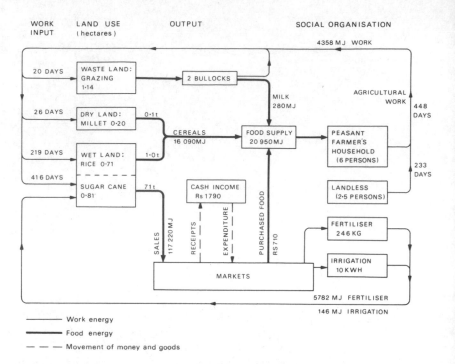

Fig. 6.5 Energy and material flows on a Middle Peasant farm, Wangala village, 1955.

——————— Work energy

━━━━━━━ Food energy

— — — Movement of money and goods

population growth), but the social transformation was substantial. In both cases a small number of rich farmers and a large pool of underemployed casual labourers were created, the one group too powerful to be controlled by government legislation, and the second too numerous, too dependent, or too indebted to be able to improve its position except through emigration.

The new agriculture in Wangala was certainly more labour-intensive, but the numbers seeking work were growing more quickly than the number of jobs—and of course the total land area available to the village did not increase at all. Scarlett Epstein estimated that in 1955 at least 30% of the population could have been completely unemployed without total agricultural production being reduced in any way. Instead, no one was unemployed but the majority were underemployed, and many (especially the one-third belonging to Servant Castes or Untouchables) were poor to the extent of suffering malnutrition. We have here a clear-cut case of relative overpopulation, but since there were few opportunities of employment elsewhere in the region, the distress was not manifested in out-migration.

A Middle Peasant's farm

Our detailed example of energy flow comes not from the successful agrarian capitalists, nor from the landless labourers, but instead from the middle group of small Peasant Caste farmers, who in 1955 still constituted the majority of households. Scarlett Epstein collected detailed records of land-holdings, income and expenditure from several households, and it is her data for a representative middle farmer and his household that are shown in Fig. 6.5, expressed in terms of the major energy and material flows.

As with Ontong Java (Chapter 5), this agricultural system contains an important cash crop sector (sugar cane) as well as traditional subsistence production (rice and millet). The major energy subsidy is fertiliser, which is only used for sugar cane. Human labour is still a major energy input, supplemented by bullock power, especially for ploughing, carting and threshing. The bullocks need to be given some fodder, mostly non-edible items from the farm such as rice hay, millet hay or cane leaves, and they also graze on harvested fields or the village waste. A pair of buffalo cows are kept by the household for their milk, but they receive no fodder and survive entirely by their own grazing efforts, tended by women or children.

Manure from these livestock is a vital source of re-cycled nutrients for the arable crops. As in the sheep-and-corn economy of southern England (Chapter 4), it is largely the manure transfers which enable some land to be kept in productive and perennial cultivation. In this South Indian system the quantity of manure available was not, however, sufficient to allow more than one crop per year, and by modern standards the yields of paddy rice and finger millet are rather low.

In 1955 fertiliser was used almost entirely for sugar cane, and it was available only because the local sugar factory could provide it on credit as part of a contract with farmers to purchase a given acreage at a given price. Few of the middle farmers could have afforded to buy fertiliser out of their savings. When grown in this way sugar cane generates an impressive yield of food energy. Growing for the full 12 months of the year, amply supplied with water and nutrients, and efficiently photosynthesising via the C_4 pathway (see Chapter 1), sugar cane performs magnificently in the climatic conditions of South India. It is also highly labour-intensive, requiring 61% of the total human work on the farm and accounting for most of the hired labour.

Efficiency of the Wangala peasant

Even if we include in the farm its proportionate share of the village waste land, used only for rough grazing, the overall energy yield of the agricultural system is substantial: 42,280 MJ/ha/year in food energy. This is almost three times the energy yield of Ontong Java atoll, and 4–5 times the yield of pre-industrial farming in Wiltshire, and it clearly reflects the intensive use of resources for highly productive crops in a milieu where necessity dictates that all land be exploited to the full.

The GEP is also high, despite the largely pre-industrial technology employed and the underemployment of household labour. We must add to the six persons who belong to the Middle Peasant household (see Fig. 6.5) an additional 2½ casual labourers, the number which on average would be supported by the 368 rupees paid by the farmer in wages (Epstein's data for Untouchables show that on average one person subsisted off 150 rupees in cash income). These 8½ persons generated per caput 44.1 MJ per day, a level intermediate between Ontong Java and pre-industrial Wiltshire (Chapters 4 and 5).

The overall efficiency of energy use (energy ratio) is less favourable, owing to the energy subsidies, especially fertiliser, which make up 58% of the total input. (This is calculated using Gerald Leach's (1976) data for ammonium nitrate and phosphate fertiliser, assuming they are used on a 50:50 basis). Another energy subsidy is irrigation, but since in this area it derives from canals, rather than tube wells, it is not a major consumer of energy. Using data from the Punjab, we can estimate the average energy cost as 96 MJ per hectare irrigated by canal.

The energy ratio can therefore be found as follows:

$$\text{Energy ratio} = \frac{\text{Sugar cane} + \text{Rice and Millet} + \text{Milk}}{\text{Work} + \text{Fertiliser} + \text{Irrigation}}$$

$$= \frac{117,220 + 16,090 + 280}{4,358 + 5,782 + 146} \quad \text{MJ per farm}$$

$$= 13.0$$

This is a similar level to our other semi-industrial system, Ontong Java (Chapter 5).

Surplus energy income: peasant farmer

Most revealing of all, perhaps, is the surplus energy income (SEI). Epstein's household surveys provide us with the data for calculating how much of the energy produced by farmers constitutes a real surplus. The average Middle Peasant farmer aims to be almost self-sufficient in rice and millet, but he must supplement these staples with some purchases, particularly vegetables, spices, oil, butter and (occasionally) meat. Knowing (a) that the regional diet provides on average 9.57 MJ per person per day, and (b) that a typical Wangala household consumes food worth 200 rupees per caput per year, we can calculate that one rupee will purchase 17.47 MJ in food energy. The farmer's net annual income after all outlays in agriculture have been accounted for (e.g. wages, fertiliser costs, bullock hire, land tax), and after he has bought his household's food supply, amounts to 1,080 rupees, or the equivalent of 8.6 MJ per person per day in SEI.

Surplus energy income: Untouchables

If we consider the other side of the coin, however, it is clear that this healthy SEI level is made possible through the exploitation of the labour of the poor, most of whom are Untouchables with tiny land-holdings or no land at all. In Wangala each Untouchable household owned on average 0.62 ha, mostly unirrigated, which for a family of six would supply less than a third of its subsistence needs. To purchase the remainder of its food at the Middle Peasant standard (17.47 MJ per rupee) would cost 123 rupees per caput, yet Epstein's surveys show that the total cash income of Untouchable households (mostly from wages) averaged only 207 rupees per caput! The surplus is a mere 84 rupees representing a SEI of only 4.0 MJ per person per day. In fact the household would have eaten cheaper food (millet instead of rice, no meat), and probably ate less anyway. Moreover, many farmers provided their labour with a midday meal as well as wages, so reducing the burden on the Untouchable household's food budget. The gap between the farmer's surplus energy income of 8.6 and his labourer's which approaches zero is nevertheless a stark reminder of the emerging inequalities in a semi-industrial agricultural system with insufficient land, an entrenched hierarchy of social relations, and an increasingly capitalist mode of production.

Wangala, twenty years on

The new rice varieties that were developed at the International Rice Research Institute in the Philippines first became available to farmers in India in 1966. Some of the early varieties of 'miracle rice' were not altogether satisfactory, but by the mid-1970s a wide range of good high-yielding varieties (HYVs) were being grown. It is noticeable, however, that the spread of HYVs has been less successful in the hilly areas, where irrigation depends ultimately on local rainfall, than in the flood-plains where too much water is often as great a hazard as too little. In South India HYVs were found to do extremely well in the sunny dry season, but only a few farmers could afford the technology to cultivate at this time, and in many places water is simply not available. During the cloudier monsoon season the yields of HYVs are less impressive, and since the product obtained is less palatable and fetches a lower price, market-oriented farmers often stick with the traditional varieties.

In Wangala, Mandya District, irrigation water from the canals is never available in the dry season, so that farmers are still restricted to cropping in the monsoon season only. There is a further reason for HYVs having a limited impact, and that is the problems that many farmers have in raising sufficient capital to pay for the various inputs needed in the total Green Revolution package. Scarlett Epstein found when she revisited Wangala in 1970 that farmers knew that the improved varieties of seed could increase yields of paddy, but they also knew that more inputs were required. Farmers with less than 0.8 hectares of wet land were generally unable to raise the necessary working capital to provide the additional inputs, and they were therefore obliged to continue with the traditional methods of paddy cultivation.

Our case study, the Middle Peasant farmer with 1.5 wet hectares, would have been among those able to innovate. If we assume the same land area and farm household composition as in 1955, then we can assess the impact of the Green Revolution by considering the changing inputs and outputs to the system (Table 6.1). Data on these are available for 1975–6 from a project financed by the Ford Foundation which collected records from 37 farmers, mostly intermediate in their scale of enterprise.

The 1975 data are therefore broadly comparable in coverage to Epstein's 1955 surveys, and they reveal quite substantial changes (see Table 6.1 and Fig. 6.6). In 1955 the typical Middle Peasant farm had been a dual economy, with modernised sugar cane production and traditional rice subsistence. Twenty years later a semi-industrial technology prevailed throughout the irrigated parts of the farm. Overall yields had increased as a result of the adoption of HYVs and a greater investment in purchased inputs. Both HYV rice and sugar cane were now cash crops, and most of the farmer's food supply was purchased rather than home-produced.

On the other hand mechanisation was still almost non-existent. Bullocks continued to play their traditional role of providing mechanical energy at small human energy cost. Moreover, farmers in Mandya District still received all their irrigation water from canals, which are cheap and reliable but only operate for half the year, instead of investing in electric pump sets to extract irrigation water from shallow wells. As a result the benefits of HYVs were necessarily restricted, by comparison with some other regions of South India.

Table 6.1 Agricultural system of a Middle Peasant farmer in Wangala after the Green Revolution, assuming no change in farm size, land-use pattern, or the size of the farmer's household.

Land use	Input/output	Quantity (1975−6)	Energy value (MJ)	Change since 1955
Wet land				
Sugar cane	Human work	524 days	3,354	+ 26%
(0.81 ha)	Fertiliser	585 kg	12,324	+ 138%
	Irrigation	5.4 kWh	78	nil
	Sugar cane	100.2 t	165,425	+ 41%
Rice (0.71 ha)	Human work	225 days	1,440	+ 3%
	Fertiliser	166 kg	3,526	innovation
	Pesticide	7 kg	650	innovation
	Irrigation	4.7 kWh	68	nil
	Paddy	4,259 kg	43,084	+ 190%
Dry land				
Finger millet	Human work	26 days	166	nil
(0.20 ha)	Millet	98 kg	1,250	nil
Waste land				
Bullock grazing	Human work	20 days	128	nil
(1.14 ha)	Milk	(regional average)	280	nil
Farmer's household				
Composition		6 persons		nil
Subsistence food supply (millet, milk)			1,530	− 90%
Purchased food supply (rice, meat, etc.)			19,420	+ 300%
Cash income				
Farmer (net household)[a]		Rs 2,150		+ 20%
Labourer (per caput)[a]		Rs 91		− 66%
Total farm energy input			21,734	+ 111%
Total form energy output			210,039	+ 57%
Energy ratio		9.7		− 25%
Energy yield (MJ/ha)			66,470	+ 57%

[a]Using Epstein's deflation index for Wangala 1955−70 of 2.85, further deflated by 28%, the increase in rice prices 1970−76, to an overall index of 3.65. Incomes of 1975−6 are thus expressed in terms of their 1955 value.

A Middle Peasant farm in 1975

The data in Table 6 and Fig. 6.6 enable us to calculate what has been the impact of the Green Revolution on this particular farm. We should remember that the farm itself is still about modal in size for the region. but that the farmer and his household are distinctly above average in prosperity, with the landless poor an increasingly substantial fraction of the total population.

First, the effects of the Green Revolution upon the crop yields—its primary objective—have been substantial. This 3-hectare holding, only half of which is irrigated, produced in 1975 57% more food energy than 20 years previously. The total energy yield was now in excess of 66,000 MJ/ha, by far the most productive agricultural system of any that we shall consider in this book.

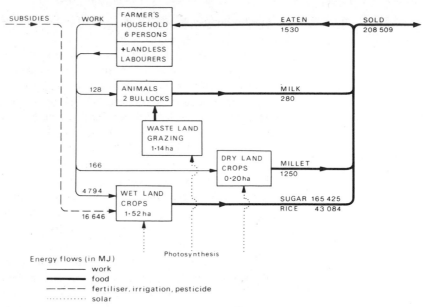

Fig. 6.6 Summary of energy flows on the farm of a Middle Peasant, Wangala, 1975–6 (in MJ per year).

This increased yield has, however, required a 111% increase in energy inputs, partly labour and partly fertilisers, etc. As a result the overall energy ratio has fallen to 9.7, diverging still further from the efficiency level of Ontong Java, our other semi-industrial case study (Chapter 5).

The cash income of the farmer has risen substantially during the twenty years, but most of the apparent rise is accounted for by inflation. Rural prices in Karnataka (Mysore) State rose by about 365% between 1955 and 1976 (see Table 6.1), so that in real terms our farmer's net income only increased by about 20%. Not enough information is available to allow us to calculate a surplus energy income, but it seems reasonable to estimate a comparable modest increase.

One significant change is that the farmer and his family do less agricultural work than formerly, preferring to employ casual labourers instead. In 1955 65% of the farm work in Wangala was done by the farm households themselves (see Fig. 6.5). Twenty years later only 15% of the work on farms in the Mandya District was done by household labour, even though the total input had risen from 418 days per irrigated hectare to 493 days. Increasingly, the more prosperous farmers are seeing their land as a business rather than a way of life, and they prefer to keep their wives at home and send their sons away for education rather than employ them at home. There is an interesting parallel in the 'gentrification' of farmers in early nineteenth-century England, a process deplored by William Cobbett as further evidence of social stratification.

Social impact of the Green Revolution

What has accentuated this division of labour in South India has been the growth of rural capitalism, a process which the Green Revolution has hastened. The pre-existing caste structure of Indian society and continuing population growth have contributed to an increasingly desperate situation for the rural poor. The new agriculture, while it remains unmechanised, does at least provide more employment, but with

81

the labour pool overflowing with landless and/or low-caste people, the level of real wages has fallen.

In 1955 the cash income of Untouchable households in Mandya District averaged 151 rupees per caput. Fifteen years later Scarlett Epstein found that these people, who are not even the poorest in the village, had in real terms seen their total incomes decline by about one-third. Many Untouchable households had had to sell their tiny plots of land, and the real value of their wages had declined. Data for 1975 are not available, but it is clear that in the 1970s the same trends continued.

As a result, the overall gross energy productivity of the sample farm has actually declined over this period, from 48 to 36 MJ/person-day. The farmer has become more prosperous, but only because he has been able to employ a much larger work-force than before and so has been able to harness the Green Revolution technology.

There are many farmers in the Wangala region who have much less than 1.5 irrigated hectares, and like the landless labourers these people have also seen little benefit from the Green Revolution. In North Arcot District in the neighbouring state of Tamil Nadu, where conditions are similar to those in Mandya District, the social impact of the Green Revolution for the less fortunate is summarised by R. Chambers and B.H. Farmer (1977) as follows:

'In North Arcot ... the very small cultivators and the agricultural labourers are trapped. If a new technology or mounting population pressure displaces them they have no chance of becoming small cultivators elsewhere ... The prospect for many of the landless scarcely bears contemplation. Extruded from the bottom of the pile, forced in desperation to leave their villages, they will swell the numbers of urban migrants and of rural transients whose lot will be more terrible for being so often unseen and so easy to avoid seeing.'

To prevent this process from continuing, a reduced rate of population growth is one measure which seems unavoidable, but without improved living standards it will be difficult if not impossible to achieve. But such improvements cannot come about simply through welfare measures, such as rice hand-outs to the urban unemployed, and some would argue that a political revolution and a social reorganisation along Maoist guidelines is the only long-term answer. One thing is certain: the Green Revolution is not revolutionary enough.

7 Full industrial systems
1: A Russian collective farm

Rural inequality: Lenin's problem

The social changes noted in the previous chapter are not inevitable consequences of 'development'. In South India the transition from pre- to semi-industrial farming technology does seem to have led inexorably to a widening in the gap between rich farmers and landless labourers, but such changes are not necessarily associated with the availability of energy subsidies to agriculture. An increase in social stratification can, in fact, occur at any technological level above basic subsistence, as the example of English farming before the Industrial Revolution showed (Chapter 4).

A recognition of the artificial nature of the inequalities in agriculture was one factor behind the growth of political protest in the nineteenth century, of which William Cobbett's writings were an early symptom. In general, however, the most influential writers (Karl Marx, Friedrich Engels) paid much more attention to manufacturing industry and the urban proletariat. Anarchists like Peter Kropotkin had a better understanding of the peasant economy, and had developed socialist policies for its reorganisation into communes. Even so, the efforts of the Anarchists to politicise the peasantry were scarcely more successful than those of the Communists.

After the October Revolution of 1917 the Russian peasants therefore constituted a major problem for Lenin. No one in the Communist Party had given serious thought to the practical question of how 25 million peasants and a pre-industrial form of agriculture were to be managed. It was, however, clear that some form of state intervention was needed, both to ensure a food supply for the towns and to prevent the growth of rural capitalism. Most of the large estates in the Russian countryside had already been seized by the peasants and split up into small farms. Inevitably, some of these new holdings were larger than others, and in any case there already existed an emerging class of richer peasants *(kulaks)*, who acted as small-scale tradesmen and employers of surplus rural labour. The kulaks were probable fore-runners of the English type of yeoman farmer, whose rigid control over rural land and labour we have already examined for early nineteenth-century Wiltshire (Chapter 4).

These emerging entrepreneurs of the Russian countryside were politically unacceptable to the new regime, but more immediately serious was the problem of food supply. The drive to rapid industrialisation required a dependable surplus from agriculture, at low cost to the state; but at the low prices that the government set, and lacking the incentive of useful manufactured goods that could be bought in any quantity, the peasants were reluctant to produce much more than their own subsistence needs, or even to sell their surplus. New state farms *(sovkhoz)* were set up, but not on a sufficient scale to meet the new needs of the towns. By 1928 it was clear that a radically new policy towards agriculture was needed if the Revolution was not to fail.

Collectivisation: Stalin's solution

Communists at this time had a firm belief in the desirability of large-scale crop cultivation, rather than smallholdings which were felt to be inherently inefficient. There was also an ideological bias towards co-operative enterprises rather than individual ones, as the most effective means whereby capitalist tendencies could be kept in check. In Russia such large-scale co-operatives had in fact emerged spontaneously in the 1920s, but even so in 1928 only 2% of the sown area was under any sort of co-operative management. This, and bread famine, was the situation which faced Stalin when he became leader of the Party following Lenin's death.

The paroxysm which convulsed the Russian countryside in the following decade has been described many times. In the four-year period 1928–32 collectivisation was forcibly extended to over 15 million peasant households, or 59% of the rural population of the USSR. By 1940 almost 19 million households were operating within the collective farm, or *kolkhoz*, system. In that year only 10% of the agricultural area was still being cultivated on an individual basis, mainly in the form of small private plots that were allowed to the peasants on collective farms as a compromise concession.

In the early years opposition to collectivisation was considerable. Most of the peasants probably regarded the Revolution as having ended in a satisfactory way with land redistribution in 1917. Their response to Stalin's ruthless measures is described as follows by the historian Erich Strauss (1969):

'Millions of peasants retaliated, partly by sporadic acts of violence but mainly through killing off their livestock . . . The main weapon of the peasants in the struggle was passive resistance, mainly in the form of sullen refusal to work effectively on the newly formed collective farms and to hand over their means of production to them . . . The struggle reached its grisly climax in the winter of 1932–33, when a man-made famine swept parts of the Ukraine, the northern Caucasus and Kazakhstan; the number of victims will probably never be known but it has been estimated at 4–5 million people.'

Half a century has passed since this turbulent period in Russian history. The collective farms that exist in the Soviet Union today are in many ways quite different from the collective farms that were set up by Stalin's regime, but it is worth bearing in mind the historical reasons that lie behind their existence. Such farms are not self-regulating, autonomous systems like some that are described in this book. Instead, they are planned to fulfil a particular role within a socialist state—a role which entails certain costs as well as conferring certain benefits.

Collective farming in Russia today

Because of this controversial history, modern collective and state farms in the USSR have not always been treated objectively by Western observers. On the other hand, it is not easy for the outsider to obtain detailed information to contradict some of the myths which have been repeated. The geographer Leslie Symons (1972) comments that 'while press reports

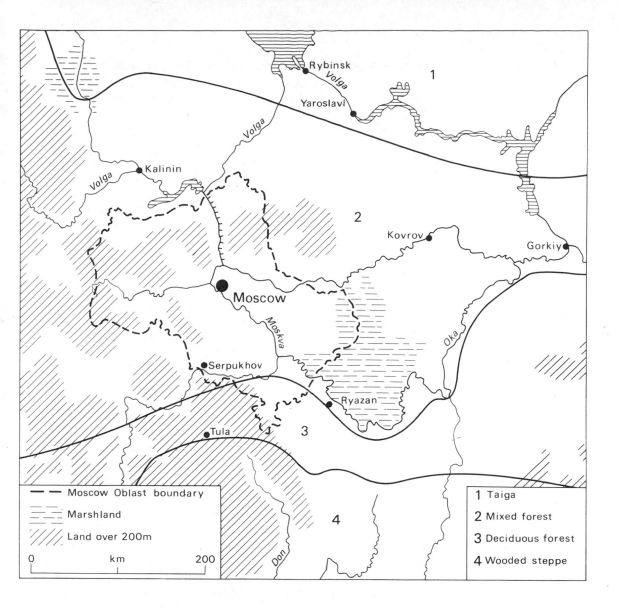

Fig. 7.1 Vegetation zones in the vicinity of Moscow Oblast.

give some insight into the workings of individual Soviet farms, they never provide comprehensive reports; similarly, it tends to be the rather exceptional farm to which foreign visitors are taken'. The only way of obtaining data from a random sample of farms is to use official statistics, and these always refer to whole regions, which are often gigantic in size and thus ecologically quite varied.

Moscow *Oblast* (Region) is one of the smallest areas for which data have been published. Even so this is a region a little larger than Switzerland (Fig. 7.1), with a rural population of 1.6 million, but of these fewer than 150,000 are associated with collective farming. The region forms the agricultural hinterland of Moscow, itself a city of 8 million people. Because of Moscow, agriculture in this region is not typical in certain respects: the city exerts a considerable influence over both land use and collective farm management.

The phenomenal growth of Moscow over the last quarter of a century has led to growing problems in the supply of food, especially perishables such as milk and vegetables. In an attempt to tackle this problem the state farms (sovkhoz) in Moscow Oblast have been greatly expanded in their size, total area, and degree of mechanisation, and the collective farms (kolkhoz) have shown a corresponding contraction. In 1940 there were over 6,000 small collective farms in this region, occupying 85% of the agricultural land. Twenty years later, in 1960, their number had fallen to 180 occupying only 14% of the area. In that year there were also 180 state farms, but their average size was much larger. These changes in the relative importance of the two sectors have continued since then, but at a much slower rate.

The data presented in this chapter were published in 1967 in a book documenting social and economic progress in Moscow Oblast during the 50 years since the October Revolution. The information is detailed, but the picture of a collective farm that one can construct is the statistical average kolkhoz of 1966, rather than a specific farm. Moreover, the information is incomplete as regards the private plots of the collective farm workers. According to Lenin this private sector should wither away when pure communism is eventually achieved in Russia, and indeed the importance of private production has declined in recent decades with improvements in the efficiency of state-run farming. Nevertheless, production from private plots continues to supply over 25% of total agricultural output in the USSR, from only 3% of the cultivated area. The private plots supply about one-third of the meat, milk and vegetables, and over half the national output of eggs and potatoes.

In Moscow Oblast the private plots of collective farm households average 0.31 hectares, some twelve times larger than the standard British allotment. Not all this area will be cultivated, since it includes orchards and also sheds for cows and pigs. In estimating the labour inputs to the private plots we have assumed that the technology and intensity of cultivation is similar to that of British allotments, where studies have shown that if 80% of the vegetables produced are potatoes, then an average energy ratio of 11.2 (food output per labour input) is achieved. Another assumption is that sales of produce from private plots provides 25% of the total earnings of collective farm workers. This general level of income supplement is confirmed by other studies, but in the absence of actual surveys it must be regarded as approximate.

Land use in Moscow Oblast

Of all the agrarian societies discussed in this book, the farmers of the Moscow region have the least favourable climatic and soil resources. In its latitude, Moscow lies far to the north of the limits of agricultural settlement in central Canada, and it is only the ameliorating effect of Atlantic air masses that makes farming possible at all. The maritime influence raises winter temperatures to an average of − 10 °C (January), but also depresses summer temperatures: for example, the July average is only 18 °C. The summer, especially the late summer, tends to be the wettest time of the year, which causes problems for farmers who would prefer rather more rain in the early summer months of maximum crop growth, and rather less during the harvest period. Frosts have been recorded in every month except July and August, but on average there are 141 frost-free days per year, about the same as the number of days of snow cover.

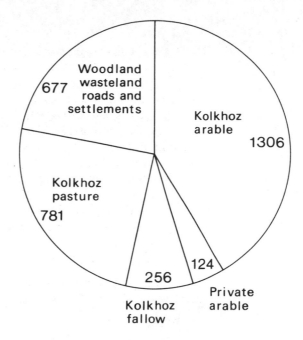

Fig. 7.2 Areas under different types of land use (in hectares) on an average collective farm in Moscow Oblast, 1966.

In this cool, humid climate the natural vegetation would be mixed spruce, pine and broad-leaved forest (see Fig. 7.1). More than half of the region remains forested, but centuries of exploitation for timber and fuel mean that virtually all the forest is secondary woodland, usually dominated by birch trees. The soils are not good: either podsols leached of plant nutrients and rather acidic, or in the poorly drained areas bog soils high in humus but low in basic minerals. If one considers the agricultural resource base, it is indeed surprising that Muscovy became the dominant state of Russia, to emerge today as the most populous and advanced region of the country. The best-adapted crops are potatoes, oats and hay, together with winter rye and barley. It is these crops which predominate today, often fed to livestock to produce meat and milk, and with an increasing production of vegetables like cabbage for the urban markets.

The average land use on collective farms in the region is shown in Fig. 7.2. The total area averages 3,144 hectares. Arable land constitutes 54% of the total, subdivided into collective arable (93%) and private plots (7%). Permanent pasture and rough grazing occupies a further quarter of the total area, and the remaining one-fifth is waste land, roads, settlements, and (mainly) forest.

Crop rotations

Crop rotations have always been an important part of Soviet agricultural planning, and for good reasons. At the time of the Revolution, most Russian peasants were still stuck in the second of the four major stages through which European arable farming has passed. These are:

1   *Shifting cultivation*, which restores soil fertility by allowing the land to revert to natural vegetation for a decade or more. On the sparsely populated frontiers of the Russian Empire this system survived into the twentieth century.

2   *Grain–fallow rotations*, often in the three-field sequence of wheat–barley–fallow. Such systems were the mainstay of medieval Europe, and survived in most of Russia until the 1930s.

3   *Legume rotations*, where grain crops benefit from the green manure of legumes like clover, and with root crops like potatoes, turnips, sugar beet or maize included. By the late eighteenth century such crop rotations had been widely adopted in lowland England, as we have seen in the case of Wiltshire (Chapter 4), but in Russia they were found only on the big estates of the landed gentry.

4   *Energy-subsidised cropping systems*, requiring inorganic fertilisers and herbicides, and allowing a virtual monoculture of the most profitable crops. The Green Revolution in tropical countries represents an attempt to transplant these energy-intensive practices into a pre-industrial milieu (Chapter 6).

In 1966 the following rotation would have been followed by most collectives in Moscow Oblast:

Year 1   Wheat.
Year 2   Potatoes or fodder crops (maize, sunflowers).
Year 3   Barley or oats, with a permanent grass–clover mixture sown simultaneously.
Year 4   Grass with clover, for hay.
Year 5   Grass with clover, for hay and summer grazing.

In the sixth year the land was sufficiently recovered for wheat again to be sown. It is worth noting the livestock bias in this arable system: for 3–4 years out of five, the net primary production of the land is being channelled to animals, either in the form of harvested crops (fodder, barley, hay), or through direct grazing.

The geography of manure

As in pre-industrial England, animal manure is vital to the success of this rotation. Manure comes direct from the grazing animals (in Year 5), and also indirectly through transport from the farmyard in Years 1 and 2 (Fig. 7.3). Typically, the wheat received up to 1 tonne per hectare of manure, and the potatoes/fodder up to 4 tonnes. Inputs of chemical fertiliser were restricted to the wheat crop.

This crop rotation would have been followed on most of the land with poorer podsol soils and on land geographically remote from the sources of labour and manure. It corresponds to the practices in the 'outfield' sector of pre-industrial farming in Britain. The land closer to the settlements, the 'infield' category, received more manure and more labour, and the rotations here usually included vegetables such as cabbages, and excluded the two years of grass cover which are unnecessary if there is heavy manuring. However, the most lavish application of inputs would be reserved for the private plots of the collective farm workers, which are even closer to home and so receive constant care and attention, not to mention abundant manure and compost (Fig. 7.3).

In 1966 the average collective farm in Moscow Oblast possessed 40 tractors and 4 combine harvesters, but by comparison with the state farms

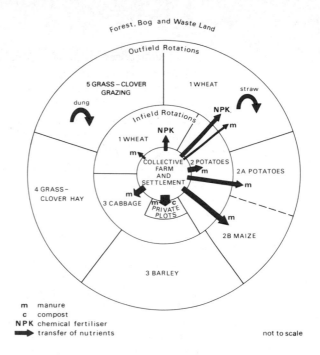

Fig. 7.3 Idealised map of land-use zonation on a Moscow Oblast collective farm.

m   manure
c   compost
NPK chemical fertiliser
➤   transfer of nutrients

not to scale

they still relied quite heavily on manual labour. On such large land-holdings much time would be wasted if the crops requiring most hand labour (e.g. cabbages, potatoes) were not located close to the settlement. Since there has also been a tendency on Russian collectives for outlying hamlets to be abandoned, and for more and more people to live in the central settlement, it becomes sensible for the spatial organisation of land use to be zoned in the way suggested in diagrammatic form in Fig. 7.3. The second reason for this zonation is that other inputs such as manure also incur a transport cost, especially in the so-called 'seasons of roadlessness' of spring and autumn, when farm roads tend to become seas of mud. In Russia we can therefore still see traces of the land-use pattern which was analysed by von Thünen in Prussia in the early nineteenth century, but in the Soviet case it is central planning rather than market forces which supplies the principal rationale.

How is kolkhoz farming organised?

Who makes the decisions about what pattern of land use to establish on a collective farm, and what type and amount of inputs to apply? In principle, each kolkhoz is still a cooperative which owns its land and the production from it, so that provided it meets its state procurement quota it is free to plant and organise in the way that it thinks best. In practice, however, the amalgamation of the small, village-based collectives into much larger units has been accompanied by an increased role in kolkhoz management for personnel trained by the state. Indeed, the difference between collective farms and the state farms (which are run like state factories) has been much reduced.

There are at least four levels of decision-making which determine the pattern of land use on collective farms. At the *state level*, procurement quotas are set for each farm, based on national needs (for example, the milk and vegetables needed by Moscow) and on what yields are thought to be attainable if farms use the recommended levels of input. At the *farm level*, the management committee decides how to fulfil this quota, and so decides what crop rotation to adopt, which fields to plant, and in what order. Thirdly, day-to-day activities are usually delegated to a *work brigade*, which is responsible for particular crops, for livestock, or for a particular part of the farm—some farms being very scattered and including more than one village. Finally, all decisions concerning the private plots (except their actual size) are the concern of individual *households*, with the women traditionally playing the more prominent role.

Conflict emerges between these different decision-making levels when the state attempts to impose unreasonable demands on the collective, as a result usually of a national policy (e.g. for maize production under Khrushchev) which is not appropriate to a particular region. In the USSR there is much more state interference with the detailed running of collective farms than is thought necessary in some other socialist countries, for example Romania. In the words of one Soviet writer:

'Crude shouting and directives [by agricultural officials] engender a reluctance to think. Reluctance to think engenders stereotyped methods. Stereotyped methods make the harvest a helpless victim of weather conditions, weeds and pests.' (*Novy Mir*, 1965)

Observers such as Basile Kerblay (1966) feel that agricultural productivity in the USSR will not improve until this problem of excessive bureaucratic interference has been solved:

Fig. 7.5 Energy and material flows on the average collective farm in Moscow Oblast.

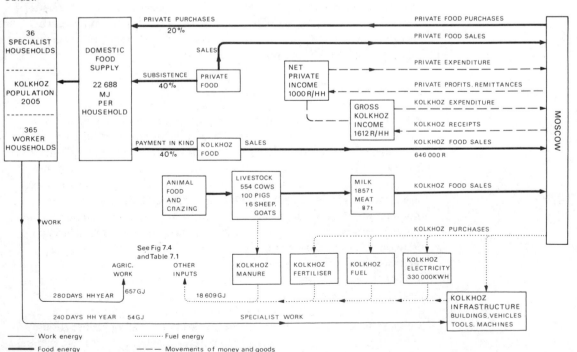

'The instinct to conserve soil fertility has deteriorated ... Furthermore, the local knowledge and experience on which the managerial prestige of the peasant was founded no longer count against the obsession of the new manager, the president of the collective farm, to obey the telephoned orders rather than the dictates of the land.'

Collective work versus private work

Energy inputs for an average collective farm in Moscow Oblast in 1966 have been analysed in terms of human labour, food output, and energy subsidies to production such as fertiliser, fuel and electricity (Figs. 7.4 and 7.5). Mechanisation and fertilisers were regarded as the main weapon in the struggle to raise the dismally low yields that had characterised the Stalinist period.

The input of collective labour amounts to 135 days per year per household, with milk production the most important sector (Fig. 7.4). This figure is low by comparison with collective farms elsewhere in the Soviet Union, partly because of the unfavourable climate of Moscow: snow lies on the ground for an average of 146 days in the winter and spring, restricting considerably the period available for outdoor work. The low work input also results from the distorted social structure of collective farm households in this region, where plentiful opportunities exist for men to find jobs in Moscow and nearby industrial towns. Urban employment usually provides more money, better housing, and higher status than collective farm work, so that in the rural hinterland of large cities old people and women tend to form a large proportion of the working population.

Fig. 7.4 Labour inputs, crops, and their harvested outputs, average Moscow Oblast collective farm, 1966.

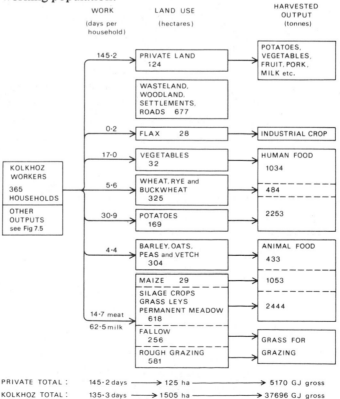

Fig. 7.6 Peasants selling honey in a market for private produce, Khabarovsk, USSR.

In addition to the collective farm work, an estimated 145 days per year per household are devoted to the private plots. The annual total for agricultural work is therefore 280 days per household, or approximately 43 hours per week.

Output: the role of private enterprise

The collective farm's output is mainly potatoes (2,252 tonnes), milk and meat (1,944 tonnes), vegetables (1,034 tonnes) and grain (484 tonnes). These products provide the state with over 20 million MJ in net food energy, but a lot more than this is produced in the form of foods such as barley, oats, peas and maize, which are potentially edible by man but which are actually fed to livestock. Inclusion of these products increases the gross level of farm output to almost 43 million MJ (see Fig. 7.4).

During this period about 40% of the diet on collective farms derived from the private plots. In addition, produce sold from these plots provided about 25% of household income. For Moscow Oblast, with an average of 401 households per collective farm, these data imply that the private plots produced about 5.2 million MJ in net food energy, or about one-fifth of the total for the collective as a whole. Since this private production derived from only 7% of the cultivated land, the continuing strength of private enterprise in Russian agriculture is very clear (Fig. 7.6).

Gross energy productivity

From these data on gross output, collective and private, we can now calculate the GEP of the collective farm population, which together includes an estimated 36 specialist households (managers, agronomists, vets, technicians and engineers) as well as the 365 worker households in the total of 401. (Ideally we would include some of the remote bureaucrats involved in farm decision-making, but we do not have the data.) Assuming on average five persons per household, the GEP is 58.6 MJ/person-day.

By comparison with our other case studies, the Russian collective generates about six times more food energy per caput than the New Guinea system, and 50% more than any of the semi-industrial systems; surprisingly, it has a lower productivity than pre-industrial farming in Wiltshire, despite partial mechanisation. One reason might be that the collective, unlike the capitalist system, does not seek to extract the maximum work from the minimum work-force. It also seeks to provide its population with a broadly equal share of the 'profits'. To what extent is it able to do so on a scale comparable to its level of productivity?

The cash income of kolkhoz workers

To discover the true situation, we cannot simply cite the egalitarian ideology of the collective farm and the average energy productivity figures given above. After all, neither the collective ideology nor the production statistics were very different under Stalin, yet for three decades the collective farm workers became in effect subsistence cultivators whose surplus labour was exploited for starvation wages to the state's benefit. What are the real returns from collective farming, given that over four-fifths of net output derives from the state sector, and therefore must be sold to the state at state prices?

In 1966 the actual income of each household would have depended on how many 'labour-day units' its members had spent on collective tasks in the previous year. Jobs requiring particular effort or skill were graded as deserving more than one labour-day unit per actual day worked. Using average multipliers, we can calculate that 135 actual working days on the collective would have generated 242 labour-day units, each worth about 3 roubles in payment. The cash return from collective farming would therefore have averaged about 725 roubles per household, some of which would be paid in kind rather than in cash. This collective income would have been supplemented by about 275 roubles derived from private produce sold in urban markets, and from remittances sent home by family members working for wages in Moscow.

The total income of 1,000 roubles per household is both an approximate and an average figure. On the other hand, although approximate it does conform broadly to the level of income reported for collectives elsewhere in Russia at this time, especially if we assume that by no means all collective households in Moscow Oblast contain more than one worker. As an average figure, it no doubt hides some variation: Leslie Symons reports that specialist workers on collective farms that he visited earn 50% more than the minimum level of earnings. However, this is considerably less that the variation in earnings that we have seen in other farming systems.

Surplus energy income

Published surveys indicate that the average Russian diet in 1966 provided in food energy 3,100 kcal (13.0 MJ) per person per day, for an average annual cost of 252 roubles. In other words, one rouble will purchase 18.77 MJ in average food requirements, so that we can say that a household income of 1,000 roubles is the equivalent of 18,770 MJ in food energy.

How much of this income really is 'surplus', in the sense of not being required for basic food purchases? Expenditure on food accounts for some 60% of total income, according to our estimates (see Fig. 7.5). Of this, about one-third is spent on meat, fish, vegetable oil and occasional luxuries. Two-thirds consists of payments in kind from the collective in the form of bread, which is a major item in the diet.

The surplus energy income is therefore only about 40% of the 18,770 MJ per household per year, in other words 4.1 MJ/person–day. For those who would like to believe in the benefits achievable under modern collective farming, this figure compares rather disappointingly with those for other farming systems:

	MJ/person–day
Maring, New Guinea 1962–3 (total population)	2.3
Wiltshire 1826 (labouring class)	2.4
Ontong Java atoll 1970–1 (total population)	5.3
South India 1955	1.8–7.5

The Russian figure is, of course, depressed by the artificial nature of prices in the Soviet Union. If the collective farm workers could sell all their produce on the free market, then their incomes would be considerably higher and their surplus energy incomes correspondingly improved.

Furthermore, Soviet writers often make the point that a number of fringe benefits are available to collective farm workers, such as free holidays, subsidised cultural activities (theatre, cinema, etc.), and free hospitals and schools. These benefits are thought to raise the value of agricultural incomes by about 30%, if a true comparison is to be made with incomes in capitalist countries. A final point is that in the period since 1966 further improvements have taken place in kolkhoz wage levels, which now average about 150 roubles per month (over 2,000 roubles annual income). More up-to-date data would undoubtedly show a more favourable comparison of collective farm workers with agricultural workers elsewhere.

Energy yields: private enterprise, collective neglect?

There are enormous differences in yield between the intensively cultivated private plots and the collective farm land. Our data suggest almost a sixfold difference in net energy yield between the intensively cultivated private plots and the collective farm land:

	MJ/hectare
Private plots	41,590
Collective land	6,680

The difference is reduced slightly if we exclude the forest and waste from the collective land category (see Fig. 7.2), but even so there is no question but that the collective land receives less care and attention than it should.

In recent years there has been some recognition that the private plots of kolkhoz workers, like those of urban workers, are highly productive despite almost total state neglect. The Moscow newspaper *Pravda* commented in 1975:

'Let us look how the household plot is cultivated: in the main, by means inherited from the distant past. Up until now there has been no organised production of mechanical tools for market-gardening, yet such equipment is produced in other socialist countries, for instance Czechoslovakia.'

Such innovations might become more necessary in the future, not so much to raise yields which are already high, but to maintain the level of output by allowing some savings of time to be made. As average earnings have increased in the USSR, so the incentive to cultivate private plots to the full becomes less strong (just as many allotments in Britain fell into disuse in the 1950s).

The overall energy yield (collective and private land amalgamated) is 8,060 MJ/ha, a level barely above that in Wiltshire in the early nineteenth century. Soils and climate in Moscow Oblast are less favourable, but the comparison of private plots with collective land shows that the Russian system still has a long way to go before it reaches its full potential.

Energy subsidies

It is not easy to assess the total energy cost of any subsidy to an agricultural system, but in this book we have drawn a boundary around each system at the 'farm gate'. We have considered only the direct inputs and outputs across this boundary. The convention provides at least a consistent way of viewing each system's efficiency.

Whereas in pre-industrial systems human work is the principal input, with industrialisation this input is increasingly dwarfed by the magnitude of other energy sources used to supplement human effort. In the case of Moscow collectives in 1966 (see Table 7.1), the process has gone far beyond the modest subsidies that we saw used by Polynesian islanders and Indian rice farmers (Chapters 5 and 6).

In Moscow Oblast, mechanisation of tasks which the peasants formerly carried out by hand or with the help of horses accounts for almost half the subsidy, through the need for fuel and machine maintenance. The rest of the subsidy is accounted for by the inputs of fertiliser, which together with manure replenish nutrient cycles so as to eliminate altogether the need for fallow land, and by electricity.

Electricity consumption is often quoted by Soviet planners as an index of rural modernisation, and in the mid-1960s Moscow Oblast was well ahead of the national average in this respect. Whereas the national average was just under 30 kWh per agricultural worker, the figure in Moscow Oblast was over 800 kWh. Contrast this, however, with the UK figure (1965) of almost 5,400 kWh per full-time agricultural worker, and the still labour-intensive nature of Russian agriculture immediately becomes plain. As an energy input per unit area, there is much less difference in electricity consumption between British and Moscow farms. For England and Wales, Gerald Leach has calculated that in 1970 mixed farms with significant dairying (similar, therefore, to those in Moscow Oblast) had an average energy input in electricity of 3.34 GJ per hectare. The Moscow figure for 1966 is 3.16 GJ/ha (collectively cultivated land, excluding waste).

From the data shown in Fig. 7.5 and Table 7.1 we can now calculate the overall energy ratio:

Table 7.1 Energy subsidies into collective farming: statistical basis of estimate for Moscow Oblast, 1966.

Item	Quantity needed	Conversion factor	Energy Input (GJ)	Proportion of total
Fuel				
Diesel @ 108 kg/ha, all crops	95.8 t	51.7 MJ/kg	4,953	27%
Lubricating oil @ 29 kg/ha, all crops	25.7 t	49.0 MJ/kg	1,259	7%
Depreciation and repairs				
40 tractors, 4 harvesters, etc.	—	43% of fuel energy needs	2,671	14%
N Fertiliser				
Cereals @ 60 kg/ha	37.7 t	26.2 MJ/kg	988	5%
Vegetables, potatoes, flax and fodder crops @ 120 kg/ha	31.0 t	26.2 MJ/kg	812	4%
P and K fertiliser				
Cereals @ 140 kg/ha	88.0 t	19.8 MJ/kg	1,742	9%
Vegetables, potatoes, flax and fodder crops @ 240 kg/ha	72.3 t	19.8 MJ/kg	1,432	8%
Electricity				
Farm and domestic use	330,000 kWh	14.4 MJ/kWh	4,752	26%
All energy subsidies			18,609	100%

Sources: (a) Items: diesel fuel and oil: Milyavsky 1967, pp. 15 and 31, using data for total fuel costs in maize cultivation; vehicles and electricity consumption: Moskovskaia Oblast 1967; fertiliser: Dr V. Zvorykin, Moscow State University (personal communication), assuming 30% N and 70% P and K (British average); (b) Conversion factors: Leach 1976.

$$
\text{Energy ratio} = \frac{\text{Food eaten} + \text{collective sales} + \text{private sales}}{\text{Work} + \text{total subsidies}}
$$

$$
= \frac{3{,}458 + 20{,}184 + 1{,}712}{711 + 18{,}609} \ \text{GJ}
$$

$$
= 1.3
$$

Needless to say, this figure compares very unfavourably with all our previous examples. The application of industrial technology to food production, involving as it does massive injections of fuel, fertiliser and electricity, achieves an increase in yields, cultivated area, and/or a reduction in the numbers employed, but it does so at the cost of a huge decrease in energy efficiency. Of course the cheapness of the energy subsidies, which are based mainly on the burning of fossil fuels, ensures that the wasteful use of energy in modern farming methods is hidden from view.

A stable system?

By itself, an ecological perspective on Soviet agriculture can tell us rather little about the stability or otherwise of the system. Certainly, Russian farming must adapt to environmental imperatives, for example the heavy nutrient demands of podsol soils, the inherently modest crop yields obtainable in cool, short growing seasons, and the heavy energy demands of farms where livestock need to be kept warm in the long winter. On the other hand the precise configuration of land use, the size of farm unit, and the organisation and remuneration of the work-force are all the result of political decision-making. In the case of collective farms in Moscow Oblast, decision-making happens to be local in the geographical sense, but nevertheless very far removed from any direct connection with any particular farm.

Agricultural planning in the USSR must be strongly influenced by the reality of the Russian environment, but in a highly centralised and bureaucratised state this influence is necessarily indirect. The rationale for each collective farm is defined by its role in helping to fulfil national plans, and the farm population has little scope for displaying personal initiative except in the management of its private plots. Any response by farmers to signals from their environment must, in all important respects, be made with reference to instructions from a remote bureaucracy—instructions which cannot possibly foresee all the local vagaries of weather, disease, and soil conditions.

In relation to its fantastically ambitious goal, the achievement of Soviet agriculture has perhaps been remarkable. On the other hand, our energy analysis of Moscow Oblast collective farms (themselves amongst the most modern in the USSR) does not suggest that its achievements in boosting production, farm worker's welfare, or efficiency have, so far, been other than moderate.

8 Full industrial systems 2 : Wiltshire in the 1970s

The Industrial Revolution in the English countryside

In Russia, as we have seen (Chapter 7), agriculture was very largely by-passed by the Industrial Revolution until well into the twentieth century. In one sense this was also true of Britain, but in other ways we can identify some very substantial changes in farming which had occurred as indirect effects of industrialisation, or of the new attitudes to land and labour that were associated with that change. In Britain, the concentration of land ownership into the hands of a few individuals; the conversion of farm workers into a landless, rural proletariat, albeit one almost devoid of political organisation; and the increased dependence of agriculture on urban markets which the growing network of canals, railways and roads made possible: these were all changes that were under way by the 1820s (see Chapter 4), and had by themselves led to an enormous structural transformation of rural society.

Nevertheless, in the narrower technological sense British farming, like that of Russia, was essentially pre-industrial at the turn of the century. Very little fossil fuel was consumed in growing food. Most of the energy consumed was provided by over one million farm workers and by an even larger number of horses. In 1901 there were 3.5 million horses in Britain of which 1.1 million were employed on farms and the rest mostly in off-farm transport, including the transport of farm produce. Gerald Leach (1976b) has estimated that about 30% of the lowland farm area was devoted to the keep of horses. He also comments that in 1900 'oxen were still in use, and farmers' accounts show that a well-driven team pulling a single plough would turn over about 0.4 hectares each day—much the same as in Saxon times a thousand years before'.

Today it needs much more imagination to trace such great continuity in farming methods across the millennia. In the space of 50 years British agriculture has proceeded through the semi-industrial stage that I have described elsewhere in the world (Chapters 5 and 6), and has entered the full industrial age. Whether or not full industrial farming systems are viable in the long run is one of the major questions that will face not only farmers, but mankind in general, in the twenty-first century. In this chapter we shall examine how these systems function by comparison with those that preceded them.

Despite industrialisation, the apparent continuity of life in the English countryside is still very strong. Although some of their fields have been amalgamated into larger units, farmers in Wiltshire still operate today within field boundaries which in some cases extend back to Saxon or even Roman times. Medieval cottages still survive in villages like Milton Lilbourne, although no doubt the hovels of the former labourers have mostly collapsed into oblivion (Fig. 8.1). The nucleated village settlements strung out along the spring line of the chalk escarpment in the Vale of Pewsey still have links with local market towns such as Devizes. On the

surface little has changed. In energy terms, however, the transformation of agriculture could hardly be more complete.

Present-day land use in Milton Lilbourne

So that we can maintain the micro-scale focus which is appropriate for an understanding of agricultural systems, let us briefly consider the changes in farming that have occurred in central Wiltshire, as exemplified by Milton Lilbourne parish. Change in the pattern of land use is one piece of evidence that we can use (Table 8.1). On the surface little has changed, apart from a decline in the total area used for agriculture. In 1840 (year of the Tithe Survey) 86% of the parish was classed as arable land or pasture, whereas the Ministry of Agriculture's statistics show that in 1977 only 62% was in these two categories.

Table 8.1 Land use in Milton Lilbourne parish, Wiltshire, 1840 and 1977.

Land use	1840	1977
Arable (including grass leys)	66%	46%
Permanent grass	20%	16%
Non-agricultural (woodland, park built-up area, roads, wastes)	14%	38%
Wheat		122 ha
Barley, oats		243 ha
Fodder crops	963 ha	10 ha
Leys		281 ha
Other arable		20 ha
All grass	approx. 620 ha	418 ha

Sources: Tithe Commutation Survey 1840 and Ministry of Agriculture 1977.

Two main factors account for this reduction. One has been an expansion in the non-agricultural and built-up area in and around the village of Milton (although the total population has in fact declined). Secondly, some land on the bare chalk hills bordering the Vale of Pewsey has been planted with conifers, much of it during the agricultural depression of the late nineteenth century. The 1880s in particular were a time of very low prices for grain, beef and mutton, as cheap imports from the New World and the colonies began seriously to undercut the home producers. It was during this period that the sheep-and-corn economy of the English chalklands began to decline. Sheep became less profitable, and their manure was becoming less essential for the arable land as inorganic fertilisers became available to replace it. Instead, dairy farming was introduced, in response to the market provided by the growing size and affluence of the urban population of Britain, and the accessibility of the towns as a result of improved rail and road transport.

By the 1970s dairy farming had become predominant in the Vale of Pewsey. Four of the five main farms in Milton Lilbourne parish are now classified as 'specialist dairy' the other is 'arable, mainly cereals'. Barley is the major arable crop, followed by wheat. The arable land is usually rotated with grass–clover leys. Permanent grassland is restricted to a few meadows close to the farms and to downland too steep to plough—i.e. most of the chalk escarpment. Some of the barley is used on the farms as a cattle feed, and kale is also grown as fodder, but there is now no sign of the turnips and swedes which were such a mainstay of crop rotations in William Cobbett's day.

Man, animals and the recycling of nutrients

The population of Milton Lilbourne has declined in the 150 years since William Cobbett's visit, mainly because of the increasingly capital-intensive nature of modern farming. There are fewer and fewer jobs available in agriculture, and in small rural villages like Milton there is virtually no alternative employment, so that young people must increasingly migrate elsewhere to find work.

From Table 8.2 we can see that there was agricultural employment for 116 households in 1831, but for only 28 in 1971. Whereas about 86% of the parish was involved in agriculture in 1831, only about 20% was involved in 1971. In the six years that followed, the agricultural labour force shrank from 36 to 29 persons, of whom seven were wives of farmers or casual workers, and therefore only employed on a part-time basis. Particularly in the last 30 years machines have replaced manpower on a massive scale.

The size of holdings has also increased: the 11 farms of over 20 hectares which existed in 1840 have been amalgamated into only five holdings today. Animals are also less numerous (see Table 8.2). Horses have of course disappeared altogether from farms, at least as working animals. In the old sheep-and-corn economy over 4,000 sheep were kept in the parish, but these have been totally replaced by fewer than 1,000 cattle, mostly dairy cows. Unlike the sheep of former times, the cows kept today on Wiltshire farms are not wholly dependent on local resources, and in the winter months, particularly, they live to a large degree on purchased feeds.

Table 8.2 Man and animals in Milton Lilbourne, 1831 and 1971.

Category	1831	1971
Man		
Total population	660	469
Number of households	129	149
Number of households directly dependent on agriculture	116	28
Proportion of population directly dependent on agriculture	86%	20%
Number of full-time farmers	12	6[a]
Number of farms over 20 ha in size	11[b]	5[a]
Animals		
Sheep	approx. 4,400	0
Cattle	few	904
Working horses	approx. 60	0
Poultry	few	365

Sources: Census of 1831 and 1971; Ministry of Agriculture 1971 and 1977. See also Chapter 3.

[a] in 1977
[b] in 1840

Just as the *food chains* that link crops, animals and man have become integrated into wider systems of food production, leading to reduced local self-sufficiency, so *nutrient cycles* in this farming system have also become more open. The nutrient transfers formerly achieved by folding sheep on the arable land where the manure was needed, are now maintained through the market economy. Purchased chemical fertilisers supplement cow manure as a means whereby cereal monocultures on the arable land can be perpetuated, and the optimum growth of pastures ensured. Ironically these chemicals include lime, which is applied to fields on the greensand located in the Vale less than a kilometre away from abandoned chalk pits which used to be quarried for the same purpose. Manure is produced in quantity by the dairy cattle, but since the animals spend much of their time in centralised cow sheds (as in Russia, Chapter 7), their dung has to be collected and spread on the fields by machine. The inorganic fertilisers are also distributed by tractor, but on steep slopes along the chalk escarpment pellets of nitrogen fertiliser are sometimes spread by aeroplane, to improve the growth of the downland pasture.

The unchanging countryside?

The apparent continuity of life in the English countryside is therefore very much an illusion. The ecology of the agricultural systems has been transformed: land use, food chains and nutrient cycles have all changed radically since pre-industrial times, and continue to change as farmers respond with increasing sensitivity to technical innovations, market trends, and political forces. Over the last 150 years the number of farmers in Milton parish has halved, and the number of farms of over 20 hectares has more than halved (see Table 8.2). Farm holdings are thus bigger than ever, and there are still great contrasts between employers and employees in the nature of their job, pay and prospects.

Rather than being owner-occupiers, the farmers themselves are very often merely the salaried employees of massive agribusinesses, set up by syndicates of investors who see the land and its production as providing a reliable return on capital and maximum security. The market to which agricultural production is geared is now national if not European in scale, and price levels are determined by decisions that are made in Brussels as much as in London. In 1826 farmers in Milton Lilbourne were already capitalist in ideology, but the technology they used was virtually pre-industrial and thus highly dependent on human labour. In the last 150 years all except the ideology have been transformed. It is the structure of social organisation in rural England, together with climate and geomorphology, that provide the only real examples of continuity.

A typical farm in Southern England

To investigate the pattern of energy flow in full industrial systems in England we can use the official statistics of the Ministry of Agriculture. Each year in June the Ministry collects data from a random sample of farms throughout the country on all aspects of farm management, but to preserve confidentiality these statistics are published as regional averages rather than as individual case studies. To coincide with the availability of other data, the year chosen for our analysis is 1971–2.

Wiltshire is located within the Southern Region of England, where the typical farm has a mixed pattern of land use but with a preponderance of cereal cropping. Barley is the principal crop, followed by wheat, with fodder crops like kale and cash crops like potatoes being of minor importance. Some land is under permanent grass, and a similar area is under temporary leys of grass planted as part of a crop rotation. The grass, the fodder crops and some of the barley are fed to livestock, which are mainly cattle but include a few sheep and poultry. As we have seen, Milton Lilbourne has a greater dairy farming component than is typical of the Southern Region, but otherwise its land use is very similar.

In Fig. 8.2 is shown the energy flow on a farm of 460 hectares, which is three times larger than average but quite close to the median size of holding. Fig. 8.2 is thus directly comparable with Fig. 4.7, which shows Fyfield Manor Farm (also 460 hectares) in the year 1826. Inputs and outputs have been converted into energy terms using the data provided by Gerald Leach in his book *Energy and Food Production*. Leach quantifies the real energy cost per £ of the fertilisers, fuels, power, machinery, feeds and seeds that were used on farms in England and Wales in 1972. He ignores in his analysis the energy inputs provided by manual labour, because of their negligible magnitude. This is well shown in Fig. 8.2, where energy subsidies totalling 10,044 GJ completely dwarf the direct human input of 16.3 GJ of energy from human work (20,400 hours).

The energy ratio

Because English farming today is designed to maximise profits through a very thorough application of modern technology, and because all this technology has itself been developed in an era of cheap fuel, it is not surprising that the agricultural system in Fig. 8.2 is grossly inefficient in its conversion of energy. The energy ratio is computed as follows:

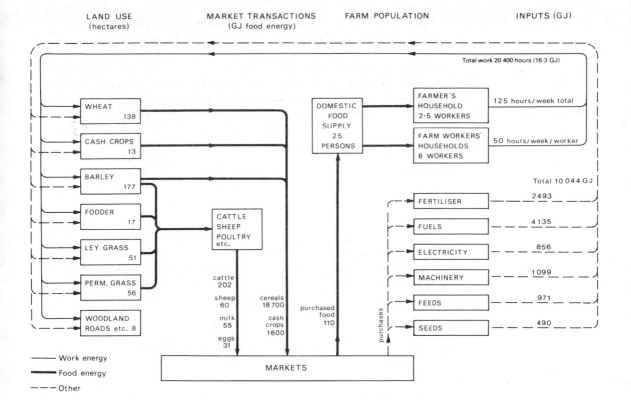

| LAND USE (hectares) | MARKET TRANSACTIONS (GJ food energy) | FARM POPULATION | INPUTS (GJ) |

Fig. 8.2 Average pattern of energy flows on a 460-hectare arable farm in Southern England, 1971–72.

$$\text{Energy ratio} = \frac{\text{Crops sold} + \text{animal products sold}}{\text{Work input} + \text{total subsidies}}$$

$$= \frac{20{,}300 + 348}{16.3 + 10{,}044}\text{ GJ}$$

$$= 2.1$$

This farm is less profligate in energy use than the Russian collective (Chapter 7), mainly because of its smaller livestock component. Nevertheless, the typical arable farm of Southern England is very inefficient in output : input terms when we compare it with less industrialised systems. Other types of farming in Britain are comparable in their efficiency ratio, as Gerald Leach (1976b) has shown:

Type of enterprise	Energy ratio
Specialist dairy farms	0.3–0.5
Mainly dairy farms	0.3–0.8
Cattle and sheep	0.4–1.2
Pigs and poultry	0.3–0.4
Cereals	1.9–2.4

These figures show that farms specialising in animal products, where the crops (if grown) are mainly fed to livestock and hence are transformed very inefficiently into human food, are generally consuming a lot more energy than they actually produce. This situation is relatively new: for the UK as a whole, Leach (1976b) found that between 1952 and 1972

'While the labour force declined by 50%, the energy input per man rose at phenomenal rates, more than tripling during the period. In 1972 each full-time worker was backed by a *direct* energy input of 502 GJ or 11.2 t of oil equivalent per year ... This put agriculture well into the category of heavy industries ... The worker normally associated with the power-hungry machine of the factory and production line is backed by no more energy than the man who tills the fields or tends the cows.'

For this reason, the energy crisis that will face industrialised countries as their oil supplies diminish is as much a crisis of agriculture as it is of transport or of manufacturing industry.

Energy yields and productivity

The motive for the industrialisation of agriculture becomes clear when we consider the energy yield and energy productivity of this kind of farming. In Southern England the net energy yield amounts to 44,890 MJ/ha, which represents a sixfold increase on the level in Wiltshire 150 years previously (Chapter 4), and over three times the level on Moscow Oblast collective farms (Chapter 7).

The labour productivity of full industrial farming is even more spectacular. In 1971 the 460-hectare farm was managed by one farmer and his family (2½ full-time workers) employing only six supplementary workers, which represents a total dependent population of about 25 persons. (About the same number again are being supported elsewhere in the economy, through farm expenditure in manufacturing, retailing and service industries.) Dividing the gross farm output by the on-farm population gives us a gross energy productivity of 2,420 MJ per person per day, an extraordinary sixtyfold increase on the productivity of farms in Wiltshire in 1826, or indeed of Moscow collectives in 1966.

One implication is that each farm worker now produces over a thousand times more food energy than he and his family consume, thus enabling the entire UK population (98% of whom do not work on farms) to be supported with a large proportion of their food supply. If the UK population consumed less meat, milk and butter (as in World War II), then the country could easily become self-sufficient in food, provided, of course, that its energy subsidies to agriculture remained unaffected.

Surplus energy income

Some of these gigantic increases in yields and productivity that full industrial technology have made possible have been passed on to the farm workers. Although they are still poorly paid by the standards of manufacturing industry, agricultural workers have seen considerable improvements in their living standards in Britain in recent decades, as we can see from the finances of an average-sized cereal farm (156 hectares) in Southern England (Fig. 8.3). The data are again based on the official statistics for 1971–2, and they indicate that the farmer's net annual income was £5,784 as against the wages of his labourers which averaged £1,162—about a fivefold difference.

From data on how much money farm workers spend on food, we can calculate that £743 would have been left over after the family food bill

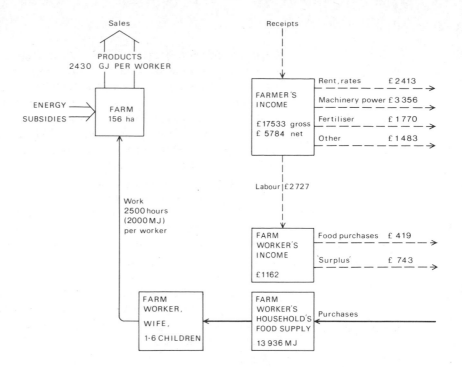

Fig. 8.3 Finances of farmer and labourer in Southern England, 1971−2.

had been paid. Since we can also calculate the energy value of the diet, we can convert this 'surplus' annual income into a food energy equivalent of 24,712 MJ, which represents 18.8 MJ per person per day (assuming 3.6 persons per household, the census average).

This surplus energy income of 18.8 MJ is between three and four times greater than any that we have encountered in previous case studies. It provides objective proof that the industrialisation of agriculture in Britain has lead to substantial improvements in welfare. In the 'bad old days' in Wiltshire, 150 years ago, each farm worker had a surplus energy income of 2.4 MJ, which was perhaps 50 times smaller than the surplus enjoyed by his employer. Today the gap has narrowed to a fivefold difference, which some would argue is still unjust, but which is certainly an undeniable improvement. The farm worker's case for a further redistribution of farm profits now rests on comparisons with the incomes of workers in other sectors of the economy, rather than on the symptoms of real hardship that were so evident in pre-industrial times.

Agriculture and the EEC

The 1970s decade ended with a further enlargement in the scale of the geographical system that directly controls decision-making on farms in Britain. The full integration of the UK into the European Economic Community has meant the extension of the EEC's Common Agricultural Policy to British farmers. The result has been the application of a policy originally designed to protect the interests of French and Italian peasants to food producers operating in a totally different social and economic context. For some two centuries now farms in Britain have been viable units of capitalist enterprise, market-oriented in their production targets, and employers of wage labour within a largely non-agricultural labour market. Through advanced technology farmers in Britain have become fully competitive even with low-cost producers of food in North America,

Australia and New Zealand. They were scarcely in need of the protection that has been provided by the EEC tariff barrier.

Urban consumers in Britain had also become accustomed to cheap food. In 1972, towards the end of the free trade era, each £1 spent on food gained on average 33 MJ in food energy. Seven years later, at the end of 1979, each £1 was purchasing only 11 MJ, a change that resulted not only from a general inflation but also from the 'harmonisation' of food prices in Britain with those elsewhere in the EEC, a process which is inevitable under the Common Agricultural Policy.

The grain harvest in Britain in 1979 was close to record levels, but much of the food that was produced is surplus to national—or even EEC—requirements. Encouraged by high Community price guarantees, farmers planted more wheat than ever before, and far more than is needed by the bakers for making bread. The standard British loaf requires a high proportion of hard wheats from North America, and despite the high EEC tariffs imposed on wheat imports the bakers find it cheaper to use American wheat, since its price on world markets is 30–40% less than the artificial price in the EEC. Much of the wheat now produced in Britain is therefore added to the rest of the grain crop (in Britain, mainly barley) in the market for animal feed, or alternatively it ends up in store. Disposing of these grain stores has recently been costing the EEC £850 million per year.

The absurdity of paying farmers high prices in order to produce surplus food which is expensive to get rid of is clear to everyone, but even so it is not going to be easy to change the Common Agricultural Policy in ways that will satisfy farmers throughout western Europe. Despite the growing unity within the EEC in certain aspects of economy and society, its agricultural systems remain diverse. For climatic as well as cultural reasons this diversity is bound to persist, even if all farmers become fully industrialised in their technology. The basic facts of agricultural geography will therefore remain an obstacle to the emergence of a government policy that will satisfy everyone when applied at the international scale.

9 Conclusions

Seven case studies cannot possibly represent the full diversity of all the farming systems that exist in the real world. In this chapter we draw some general conclusions from a comparison of this small sample of case studies (Tables 9.1 and 9.2). We should regard these conclusions as tentative, requiring in some cases to be further tested through the analysis of many more cases.

1   Although it is convenient to classify agricultural systems according to the extent of their dependence on external energy sources (pre-industrial, semi-industrial, full industrial), it is clear that within each category there is much variability in energy efficiency and social welfare. Reasons for this variability include ecological factors (soils, climate, crop type), demographic factors (population pressure), and social variables such as major differences in ideology and hence social organisation and the distribution of wealth. To fully understand patterns in agricultural geography we must adopt an integrated approach, since the patterns result from the interplay of so many different causal factors.

2   Within each region, however, the application of industrial technology does seem to result in substantial increases in energy yield, as less and less land is left fallow and as the effects of nutrient and water deficiencies are increasingly by-passed. At the same time, the proportion of this yield which is used for subsistence declines to a low level once agricultural systems develop external trading links.

Table 9.1 Summary data on inputs and outputs in seven agricultural systems, per annum.

Category, agricultural system	Energy input/hectare			Energy output/hectare	
	Total (MJ)	Percentage from work	Percentage derived from fossil fuel	Total (MJ, net)	Percentage for subsistence
Pre-industrial					
I New Guinea	103	100	0	1,460	100
II Wiltshire 1826	183	77	2	7,390	2
Semi-industrial					
III Ontong Java	1,079	43	54	14,760	10
IV S. India 1955	3,255	42	58	42,280	12
V S. India 1975	6,878	23	77	66,460	1
Full industrial					
VI Moscow collective	6,145	4	96	8,060	14
VII S. England 1971	21,870	0.2	99	44,890	0

Source: data in Chapters 3–8.

Table 9.2 Efficiency of seven agricultural systems.

Category, agricultural system	Energy yield (MJ/ha-yr)	Gross energy productivity (MJ/person-day)	Surplus energy income (MJ/person-day)	Energy ratio (output/ (input/
Pre-industrial				
I New Guinea	1,460	10	2.3	14.2
II Wiltshire 1826	7,390	80	2.4[a]	40.3 / 12.6[a]
Semi-industrial				
III Ontong Java	14,760	38	5.3	14.2
IV S. India 1955	42,280	44	8.6[b] / 4.0[c]	13.0 / 10.2[d]
V S. India 1975	66,460	36	—	9.7
Full-industrial				
VI Moscow collective	8,060	59	4.1	1.3
VII S. England 1971	44,890	2420	18.8	2.1

Source: data in Chapters 3–8.

— data unavailable.
[a] farm labourer's household
[b] Peasant Caste farmer's household
[c] Untouchable Caste household
[d] subsistence rice cultivation only

3   Between the extremes of pre-industrial self-sufficiency and full industrial capitalist farming there exists a 200-fold difference in per caput GEP. This results from the substitution of machine power for manpower on a massive scale, as well as from the energy yield improvements noted above. Farming systems that are not at these extremes vary in their productivity, but in all cases they are not far from the pre-industrial end of the spectrum. In these cases the degree of underemployment of the farming population and the role played by animal husbandry are the most important reasons for variation. The use of draft animals as 'energy slaves' will tend to boost GEP, whereas the existence of abundant leisure, either voluntary or enforced, will diminish it.

4   The real incomes of farming populations are a reflection of (a) the prevailing GEP levels, (b) the terms of trade whereby food energy is exchanged for money, and (c) the social organisation of surplus. The surplus energy income (SEI) statistic is very low in pre-industrial societies because of factors (a) and/or (c). In semi-industrial societies SEI can improve for some fortunate sections of the agrarian population, despite problems associated with factor (b). In full industrial societies SEI tends to be much higher, mainly because of huge improvements in (a). (On the other hand SEI as a proportion of GEP is lower in such societies than in pre-industrial ones.)

5   As is well known, the overall efficiency of energy use (energy ratio) diminishes as the degree of dependence on fossil fuels increases. Fig. 9.1 suggests, however, that semi-industrial systems can be almost as efficient as pre-industrial ones (energy ratio 10–40). Only in fully industrialised societies does the use of energy become so profligate that very little more energy is gained from agriculture than is expended in its production (energy ratio 1–2).

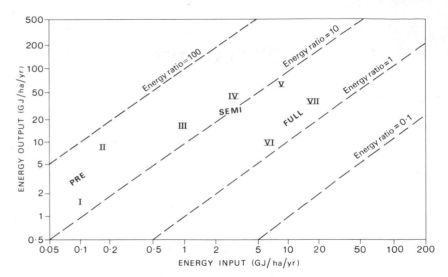

Fig. 9.1 Inputs, outputs and energy ratio: seven agricultural systems compared (I New Guinea; II Wiltshire, 1826; III Ontong Java atoll; IV Wangala, South India, 1955; V Wangala, 1975; VI Moscow Oblast collective farm; VII Southern England, 1971).

6   Perhaps, as a final conclusion, we can state that the four indices of efficiency which we have presented in this book do seem to provide a useful description of agricultural systems when used together rather than singly. The fact that we have failed to classify all aspects of agricultural systems by using the pre-/semi-/full industrial subdivision is reassuring, since there are enormous variations in ecology, population, and social organisation which the purely technological classification ignores. Farms *are* energy-consuming and energy-producing systems, and should be considered as such. However, they also provide jobs, incomes and a way of life for agrarian societies, whose social and ideological characteristics cannot be ignored.

Watanabe, I. and Lee, K.K. (1977) Non-symbiotic nitrogen fixation in rice fields. In A. Ayanaba and P.J. Dart (eds.) *Biological Nitrogen Fixation* (Wiley, London).

Chapter 7

Kabysh, S.S. (1965) The permanent crisis in Soviet agriculture. In R.D. Laird (ed.) *Soviet Agriculture: the Permanent Crisis* (Praeger, New York).
*****Karcz, J.F.** (1967) (ed.) *Soviet and East European Agriculture* (University of California Press, Berkeley). (Chapters by A. Nove, D. Joravsky, N. Nimitz, and N.M. Jasny.)
Kaser, M. (1966) (ed.) *Soviet Affairs, No. 4* (Oxford University Press, Oxford). (Chapters by B. Kerblay and W. Klatt.)
Kerblay, B. (1966). See **Kaser** (1966).
Leach, G. (1976) *Energy and Food Production* (IPC Press, Guildford).
Leversedge, F.M. and **Stuart, R.C.** (1975) Soviet agricultural restructure and urban markets. *Canadian Geogr.* **19**, 73–93.
Milyavsky, I.O. (1967) *Technologicheskie Karty i Planirovanie v Kolkhozakh* (Izdatelistvo Ekonomika, Moscow).
Moskovskaia Oblast (1967) *Moskovskaia Oblast za 50 Let Statisticheskiy Sbornik* (Statistika, Moscow).
Nove, A. (1977) *The Soviet Economic System* (Allen and Unwin, London).
Strauss, E. (1969) *Soviet Agriculture in Perspective* (Allen and Unwin, London).
*****Symons, L.** (1972) *Russian Agriculture: A Geographic Survey* (Bell, London).

Chapter 8

Central Statistical Office (1972) *Annual Abstract of Statistics 1972* (HMSO, London).
　(1970) *Social Trends No. 1, 1970* (HMSO, London).
*****Leach, G.** (1976a) The energy costs of food production. In A. Bourne (ed.) *The Man–Food Equation* (Academic Press, London).
　*(1976b) *Energy and Food Production* (IPC Press, Guildford).
Ministry of Agriculture (1973) *Farm Incomes in England and Wales No. 25, 1971–72* (HMSO, London).

Chapter 9

*****Scientific American** (1971) *Energy and Power* (W.H. Freeman, San Francisco).
　*(1976) *Food and Agriculture* (W.H. Freeman, San Francisco).
*****Bayliss-Smith, T.P.** and **Wanmali, S.** (1984) *Understanding Green Revolutions: Agrarian Change and Development Planning in South Asia* (Cambridge University Press).

112